⊲ **W9-AAQ-906**

Sales
TRAINING

Exercises, Handouts, Assessments, and Tools
to Help You:
- ✔ Create Targeted Sales Training for Both Novice
  and Experienced Salespeople
- ✔ Develop Powerful New Skills in Three Key Areas:
  Thinking, Communicating, and Networking
- ✔ Become a More Effective and Efficient Facilitator
- ✔ Ensure Training Is on Target and Gets Results

 **Press**

Jim Mikula

ASTD Press is an internationally renowned source of insightful and practical information on workplace learning and performance topics, including training basics, evaluation and return-on-investment (ROI), instructional systems development (ISD), e-learning, leadership, and career development.

Ordering Information: Books published by ASTD Press can be purchased by visiting our Website at store.astd.org or by calling 800.628.2783 or 703.683.8100.

Library of Congress Catalog Card Number: 2004109351

ISBN: 1-56286-369-X

Acquisitions and Development Editor: Mark Morrow
Copyeditor: Christine Cotting, UpperCase Publication Services, Ltd.
Interior Design and Production: UpperCase Publication Services, Ltd.
Cover Design: Ana Ilieva
Cover Illustration: Todd Davidson

Contents

Preface   vii

**Chapter 1   INTRODUCTION: HOW TO USE THIS BOOK   1
                EFFECTIVELY**

Thinking, Communicating, and Networking   1
How This Book Was Developed   3
The Context and Content of Training   3
How This Book Is Set Up   4
Basic Tips on Presenting a Class   6
How to Use This Book   8
Icons   15
What's on the CD?   16
What to Do Next   16

Chapter 2   GAP ANALYSIS AND TRAINING SALESPEOPLE   17

What Is Learning?   17
Who Should Be Trained?   19
Sales Gap Analysis   20
Tips for Training Salespeople   21
What to Do Next   23

**Chapter 3   THE BUILDING BLOCKS OF EFFECTIVE SALES   33
                PERSONNEL**

Key Points to Effective Selling   34
CD Resources   34
Selling Today Module   34
Effective Selling Module   38

Sales Cycles Module   42

Basic Knowledge Module   49

What to Do Next   55

Chapter 4   THINKING: SALES MIND FOCUS MODULE   77

Training Objective   77

Key Points in This Module   78

Materials   78

CD Resources   78

Sample Agenda   78

What to Do Next   88

**Chapter 5   THINKING: MANAGING TASKS AND   91
RELATIONSHIPS MODULE**

Training Objective   92

Key Points in This Module   92

Materials   92

CD Resources   93

Sample Agenda   93

What to Do Next   105

**Chapter 6   THINKING: CONDITIONS OF SATISFACTION   109
MODULE**

Training Objective   109

Key Points in This Module   110

Materials   110

CD Resources   110

Sample Agenda   111

What to Do Next   115

Chapter 7   PLANNING AND ORGANIZING MODULE   119

Training Objective   119

Key Points in This Module   119

Materials   120

CD Resources   120

Sample Agenda   120

What to Do Next   123

Chapter 8 **EFFECTIVE LISTENING MODULES** **131**

Artful Listening Module 132
Inquiry Module 137
What to Do Next 149

Chapter 9 **COMMUNICATING: A BASIC FORMULA MODULE** **159**

Training Objective 160
Key Points in This Module 160
Materials 161
CD Resources 161
Sample Agenda 162
What to Do Next 172

Chapter 10 **COMMUNICATING: PRESENTATIONS MODULE** **189**

Training Objective 189
Key Points in This Module 190
Materials 190
CD Resources 191
Sample Agenda 191
What to Do Next 197

Chapter 11 **COMMUNICATING: FEATURES, BENEFITS, AND PROOF MODULE** **203**

Training Objective 204
Key Points in This Module 204
Materials 204
CD Resources 205
Sample Agenda 205
What to Do Next 209

Chapter 12 **COMMUNICATING: COMPELLING OFFERS MODULE** **215**

Training Objective 216
Key Points in This Module 216
Materials 216

CD Resources		216
Sample Agenda		217
What to Do Next		224

Chapter 13	**NETWORKING MODULE**	**229**
	Training Objective	230
	Key Points in This Module	230
	Materials	230
	CD Resources	231
	Sample Agenda	231
	What to Do Next	237

Appendix A	**TRAINING PROGRAM EXAMPLES**	**243**
Appendix B	**PROGRAM EVALUATION FORM**	**246**
Appendix C	**USING THE COMPACT DISC**	**248**
	Contents of the CD	248
	Computer Requirements	248
	Printing From the CD	249
	Adapting the PowerPoint Slides	252
	Showing the PowerPoint Presentations	252

For Further Reading	254
About the Author	255

As I started writing this book, I tried to remember my very first sale. It seems as if I have been selling my entire life. Was it the raffle ticket sales in Cub Scouts or helping my grandfather at the horse auction? Growing up, I worked on our horse ranch with my grandfather. We always were busy finding buyers, "haggling" (as the horse swappers called it), talking about the benefits of the horses, and finally coming to agreements. It all was part of business, similar to keeping the books and making sure the horses stayed in prime condition. Selling was not a profession—it was the way business survived. Those down-to-earth business experiences formed my view of selling, and I am thankful—it's a simple philosophy that has served me well.

When I started my career, I ended up in sales, not because of any grand scheme or desire to be a top salesperson—I wanted to see the world. During my trainee rotation in the sales department of the first hotel I worked in, I learned that the sales people traveled often. At the end of my trainee program, I asked to be in sales. I was profoundly surprised to find that selling was not as easy as I thought. And the pressure from clients and bosses, WOW! For every victory, there were many more rejections and there always was another dead file to make a call on or the ever-present prospecting list.

Just nine months out of college, I was slogging away in sales at Hyatt Hotels with little training or support when I crossed paths with Joe Kordsmeier, who was Senior vice president of sales and marketing at the time. Joe took an interest in my career and became a wonderful mentor. He taught me about communicating and networking, and he shared many important insights with me. It didn't take too long to realize that there was no pixie dust from Joe; it was common sense: be polite, keep your promises, don't be a doormat, and understand the difference between activity and productivity. I was amazed at the relationships he developed and his proverbial Rolodex. Joe was the first sales professional I had met, and what great fortune to have him as my mentor!

Later in my career, another mentor arrived. David Neenan is the CEO of a construction company (and what CEO is not a salesperson these days?). When I met David, I was leading sales teams and training salespeople and managers. From David I learned about disciplined thinking and the art of inquiry. He showed me how to uncover conditions of satisfaction and the concerns that drive people's decision—how to exercise impeccable listening. I have learned that this is much more meaningful than overcoming objections, which is much like having a tennis match with a customer. These skills in disciplined thinking and inquiry lead to a collaborative process with clients that results in satisfied customers and sustainable relationships.

What I have learned from haggling for horses to selling luxury services is simple. There are three skills that salespeople always use: thinking, communicating, and networking. This book is intended to help you get new salespeople up to speed and productive quickly and help you provide experienced salespeople with opportunities to sharpen their skills. This book will give you an effective response to the age-old declaration, "Our salespeople need training!"

In addition to Joe and David, I would like to acknowledge the man who started me on the path that led me to this book, Claude Rand. After World War II Claude helped open up TWA offices in Europe and Asia. During his career he visited more than 130 countries. Alzheimer's disease has trapped his wonderful memories of far-away lands and people, but this book truly is his legacy. Many of the discoveries I share in this book were made because of Claude, and I will be eternally grateful for them.

Special thanks goes to Todd Lapidus and Ruth Ann Hattori of Customer Contact Corporation, or C^3 as we call the firm. Todd's patience with my multiple meanderings about what the book should really focus on and his gentle coaching were tremendous help. Ruth Ann took on the incredible task of making sure I was making sense. Her many hours of reviewing manuscripts and asking, "Are you sure you really want to say this?" have made this book much better than I ever could do on my own! Thanks, Todd and Ruth Ann; your support is wonderfully appreciated.

Finally, I would like to dedicate this book to my grandsons, Logan and Kyle, and my granddaughter Andreya Pimley! They are the essence of energy, persistence, and charisma—quite a formula for future success!

Jim Mikula
August 2004

Introduction: How to Use This Book Effectively

What's in This Chapter?

- A look at the three key elements of selling: thinking, communicating, and networking

- An explanation of how this book was developed

- Basic tips on presenting a sales training class

- A peek at what's included on the accompanying CD

Thinking, Communicating, and Networking

The essence of selling is thinking, communicating, and networking. Every customer is different, so a salesperson always is thinking about what action to take next. As soon as an action is decided on, it starts a trail of communication that continues through the follow-up process. And, along with all the active customers who salespeople must serve, they must constantly cultivate new leads through networking activities.

Every day a salesperson thinks about how to

- organize his or her day

- create compelling offers

- maintain a relationship with an existing customer

- go after more business or get more business from an existing customer

- explain the value in a new product.

This thinking is great and necessary, but are salespeople consciously aware of how their thinking affects their actions? A disciplined approach to the action they do most—thinking—might be the most important skill a salesperson can have.

In the training outlined in this book, we examine strategic thinking—a way that helps bring what goes on in the background of our minds into the foreground—so we can actively focus on becoming more effective. It can be as simple as asking oneself, "Why did I take that action, and what can I learn from it?" This practice of reflective thinking is a cornerstone for this book.

In today's busy world, salespeople engage in many forms of communication with their customers and potential customers. It is no longer possible, or at times necessary, to meet in person. Telephone and email have become the mainstays of sales communication, and both salespeople and their managers want to improve their skills. As salespeople use email and phone more often, there is a faster pace of communication and many more opportunities for miscommunication.

Taking this into consideration, many salespeople communicate with forms, standardized letters, and scripts—all with the intention of becoming more efficient. It is, literally, "push a button" and I have just communicated with my customer. The pressure of lean operations and time and performance demands all drive this need for efficiency. However, it produces generic messages and nearly anonymous communication in an environment where customers hunger to receive individual attention.

Chapters 8, 9, 10, 11, and 12 provide your salespeople with models and methods for effective listening and communicating. Email communication, which often is very frustrating to sales personnel, is covered in chapter 9 with a structured exercise.

To survive and thrive, your business must be constantly nourished with new customers. Keeping the pipeline full requires relentless effort from the sales and marketing functions. For salespeople charged with finding new business, understanding networking takes the misery out of prospecting and cold-calling. Purposeful networking enables salespeople to have a system that feeds them leads, as opposed to the traditional prospecting, which is no fun for the salesperson and often irritates the prospect. Networking requires disciplined thinking and purposeful communications. Here is a possible description of this activity: going slow initially to help you go faster later.

The networking ideas presented here come from the principles of intentional relationship building, the theory of six degrees of separation (Milgram, 1967), and *The Tipping Point* (Gladwell, 2000). Your salespeople will learn how to create momentum finding new business and managing their network. This approach yields better results in today's customer-driven environment, where making cold calls and blitzing markets can be counterproductive and potentially damaging to a brand.

How This Book Was Developed

Three words—experience, mistakes, research—describe how this book was developed. The experience comes from a lifelong pursuit of selling, but experience doesn't count for much unless it leads somewhere. My experience led to success and learning, despite a ton of mistakes. I often felt like I was living one of Yogi Berra's quotes, "We made too many wrong mistakes." This led me to conduct research into how to become a better salesperson and then how to train salespeople. This research began in 1987 and continues today.

This book is intended to help salespeople improve in three fundamental areas--thinking, communicating, and networking—and subsequently perform better at everything they do. In addition, the training modules are designed to help you pull forth the innate abilities your salespeople have and add richness to the principles and ideas presented. The philosophy infused in this book is straightforward: people already have the capacity and ability to succeed in sales; all they need is help to bring them forward.

Most of the modules in this book will benefit both experienced and novice salespeople. You can customize as well as mix and match the modules to fit the different groups on your sales staff and the specific topics that your group needs.

The Context and Content of Training

For training to be effective, there must be some context that the participant understands. Fred Kofman (founder and president of Leading Learning Communities, Inc., an international consulting firm specializing in organizational learning and personal mastery) says that learning can only start through awareness. The gap analysis in the next chapter will help your salespeople become aware of what they want to learn or would like to improve. Without having a context to which they can relate, people in the training sessions might check out. Woody Allen used to say, "I like my body; it shows up for meetings." The same could be true for sales training.

After your sales staff identifies what they want to learn or improve, you should work on the content, which is designed to work effectively within the context of how adults learn. Following Kofman's learning formula, the next step is understanding. This requires training, reading books, or hiring a coach. Understanding often causes some type of change in habits. We all know how difficult it is to change or create a habit; it takes time, reinforcement, and perseverance.

How This Book Is Set Up

Unlike most of the other books in the series, this book is organized into general modules, which you can mix and match to suit your training needs. I have taken this approach for the following reasons:

- ◆ Salespeople like to sell and want to know how to be more effective at it. But they do not want the training to take them away from their selling for too long—thus the modules were developed so you can run one or more, based on the needs of your business.

- ◆ Mixing novice and experienced salespeople in a training session can reduce the learning for all the participants. If the content is directed at the experienced salespeople, the novice salespeople might feel overwhelmed, and the opposite can result in boredom for the experienced people. The modules enable you to run sessions that are effective for both groups.

- ◆ The modules offer flexibility and usability of this work and enable you to extract only what you need when you need it. Often salespeople need training or a refresher on a specific issue. When you can train on a topic that will assist a salesperson the day after the training, you provide the best opportunity for the participants to use their new or improved skills effectively. A simple tenet of adult learning is that adults only learn what they want to learn. The flexibility provided by this modular approach helps you take advantage of this.

Before we get into the modules, chapter 2 includes tips for training salespeople, and Appendix A includes a matrix for determining who should attend the training. Chapters 3 to 13 contain the training modules, each of which is presented in the following format:

- ◆ overview

- ◆ training objective

- ◆ key points of the module

- materials needed

- sample agenda.

This format makes it easy for you to facilitate each module, and you can use the information as the basis for creating your own customized script, with your organization's terminology and examples.

The modules are as follows:

- **Selling Today, Effective Selling, Sales Cycles, and Basic Knowledge (chapter 3):** These modules cover various aspects of selling, including value-added approaches, characteristics of successful salespeople, sales cycles as part of the business process, and product, competitor, and customer knowledge—all important topics for new salespeople to tackle prior to taking any other training module in this book. (Your current training programs may cover the knowledge a salesperson needs within your organization, and thus this module may not be necessary.)

- **Sales Mind Focus (chapter 4):** This is a key module for all salespeople to attend. It helps new salespeople start off with an effective tool; it helps experienced salespeople work on current business; and it avoids using hypothetical situations, which most experienced salespeople do not like.

- **Managing Tasks and Relationships (chapter 5):** This module touches on an important aspect of selling: relationships. With impatient customers armed with knowledge about you and your competitors, a salesperson not only has to take care of the task (providing information, sending proposals, and so forth), he or she also needs to understand the kind of relationship the customer expects.

- **Conditions of Satisfaction (chapter 6) and Artful Listening and Inquiry (chapter 8):** These modules help new and experienced sales personnel identify a customer's implicit conditions of satisfaction through the skill of asking effective questions. Implicit conditions of satisfaction are the unspoken reasons a customer buys or not, and the customer often expects the salesperson to know them.

- **Planning and Organizing (chapter 7):** This module explores how salespeople can manage their time more effectively.

- **Communicating—A Basic Formula (chapter 9):** Participants will learn a simple formula for creating effective communication, whether by phone or in writing—especially email.

- **Presentations (chapter 10):** Sometimes a salesperson has only one chance to get the business—during a key presentation. This module helps salespeople fine-tune those important presentations.

- **Features, Benefits, and Proof (chapter 11):** Customers want benefits, not features. This module helps your salespeople focus on benefits and avoid relying on features as a primary selling tool.

- **Compelling Offers (chapter 12):** Using the advocacy model, participants learn that collaborating with their customers is more effective than manipulative closing techniques.

- **Networking (chapter 13):** Participants will learn the key principles for networking—an essential element for sales personnel charged with finding new business.

Basic Tips on Presenting a Class

This section provides some basic tips for leading sales training. Each point is tied to adult learning, engages the participants, and sets the environment for using the skills presented immediately after the session. You should use these tools to enhance or add to your training toolkit because the tools work for all types of training. Setting a proper environment and getting the group aligned from the start of a training session are as important as the content and the delivery of the content.

CHECK-IN AND CHECK-OUT

For half-day sessions or longer, start the meeting with a check-in exercise and finish with a check-out exercise. During a check-in session the participants share their expectations. A day-one check-in typically includes asking the participants to introduce themselves and let the class know why they are at the training and what their expectations are. On the second or third days of training, the check-in session revolves around what the participants learned the day before and what their expectations are for the day ahead. Attendees can check in either in a prescribed order (starting with one person and going clockwise, for example) or randomly. Whichever system you choose, everyone participates—including the facilitator.

A check-out session captures the learning and any commitments made. Ask the participants to share the key points they learned during the session or what they thought was important to them. On the last day the participants should share what they learned and what they will put into practice. Attendees can check out either in a prescribed order or randomly. Whichever system you choose, everyone participates—including the facilitator.

BREAKS

As much as possible, take breaks every 55–70 minutes. This will keep the participants fresher. For full-day sessions a 1.5- to 2-hour lunch break will give the attendees time to check their email and voice mail. An alternative to a long lunch break is to start the session early and finish between 3:30 p.m. and 4 p.m. so that the attendees can have a few hours at the end of the day. This helps the salespeople feel connected to their customers during training. We all have run into a situation where you ask to speak to a salesperson and are told the person is in training all day. This is as frustrating to the salesperson as it is to the customer.

COLORS AND MUSIC

Use markers of different colors on the flipcharts and worksheets to keep people engaged. Play music as people arrive and depart. Consider playing classical or new-age music as background during working sessions. Colors and music engage the creative side of the human brain and thus promote whole-brain thinking. Playing music when a group arrives can help set the tone for the session, and it provides a nice break for the participants when played as they are leaving. Playing classical, especially baroque, music has been proven to assist learning. Sometimes baroque can be a little depressing, so new-age music can provide an alternative.

PICTURES

As much as practical, use pictures from your organization in the PowerPoint presentation. This will help customize the program and provide different visuals for the participants. Pictures also engage the creative side of the brain and promote metaphorical thinking. Another aspect of pictures has to do with memory. A picture linked with a key point can help the learner remember the point by seeing the picture or remembering where it is in a training guide.

How to Use This Book

Both experienced and novice trainers can use this book in a flexible manner because you can use many of the modules independently or group them to meet the needs of your sales personnel.

What follows here and in Appendix A are sample one-day programs and suggestions for mixing and matching sales personnel. To provide some context around the different modules, timing, and appropriate participants, Table 1–1: Sales Training Modules Matrix identifies the contents of each module, tells you what chapters they are in, states the objectives of each one, and suggests the length of time required.

NOVICE TRAINERS

A recommended method to prepare for conducting sales training is to do self-study with the Basic Knowledge module in chapter 3 and then thoroughly read all of the remaining modules. After this preparation, conduct a half-day session with novice salespeople using the example of a program for new trainers presented in Table 1–2.

If you were to start with an experienced group of salespeople or a mixed group, the example of a half-day program presented in Table 1–3 could be used.

After conducting the programs suggested above, a new trainer would be prepared to take on the presentation of the other modules.

The one module that requires proper preparation and practice is Sales Mind Focus. This module supports the other modules, and without proper preparation the session could leave the participants confused about the value of the disciplined thinking that is presented.

EXPERIENCED TRAINERS

The first step for experienced sales trainers is to conduct the gap analysis to determine the priority of modules they will present. The gap analysis points to the modules you should start with and sets up all other modules. For example, if the gap analysis shows that the sales personnel want to improve email communications, you could use one of the full-day training programs outlined in Table 1–4 and Table 1–5, or you might consider the training program examples in Appendix A.

Table 1-1

Sales Training Modules Matrix

CHAPTER	MODULE NAME	GAP ANALYSIS	OBJECTIVE	POWER-POINT SLIDES	ANCILLARY MATERIALS	DURATION OF SESSION	N	E	M
3	Selling Today		To provide the participants an overview/orientation of selling today	Yes		20–30 minutes	X		
3	Effective Selling		To provide the participants an overview/orientation of effective selling	Yes	Yes	30–40 minutes	X		
3	Sales Cycles		To provide an overview/orientation of basic sales cycles and the organization's sales cycle	Yes		30–40 minutes	X	X	X
3	Basic Knowledge	Yes	Either to provide a starting point for basic knowledge training or to supplement your existing training for product, competitor, and customer knowledge		Yes	60 minutes or more	X		

N = novice salespeople; E = experienced salespeople; M = sales management.

continued on next page

Table 1–1, continued

Sales Training Modules Matrix

CHAPTER	MODULE NAME	GAP ANALYSIS	OBJECTIVE	POWER-POINT SLIDES	ANCILLARY MATERIALS	DURATION OF SESSION	N	E	M
4	Sales Mind Focus	Yes	To provide a disciplined method for improving a salesperson's productivity	Yes		1.25–1.5 hours	X	X	X
5	Managing Tasks and Relationships	Yes	To provide insights into managing tasks and relationships effectively	Yes		Less than 1 hour	X	X	X
6	Conditions of Satisfaction	Yes	To help participants understand the concept of conditions of satisfaction and the difference between explicit and implicit conditions	Yes		1 hour	X	X	X
7	Planning and Organizing	Yes	To provide an opportunity for salespeople to examine their activities and the way they allocate their time for those activities	Yes	Yes	1 hour		X	X

N = novice salespeople; E = experienced salespeople; M = sales management.

continued on next page

Table 1-1, continued

Sales Training Modules Matrix

CHAPTER	MODULE NAME	GAP ANALYSIS	OBJECTIVE	POWER-POINT SLIDES	ANCILLARY MATERIALS	DURATION OF SESSION	N	E	M
8	Artful Listening	Yes	To provide insights into effective listening	Yes	Yes	30–40 minutes	X	X	X
8	Inquiry	Yes	To improve the inquiry skills of the participants so that they can get their customers to comfortably disclose important information, such as implicit conditions of satisfaction	Yes	Yes	1.25–1.5 hours	X	X	X
9	Communicating—A Basic Formula		To provide a formula that can be used for all communications, with emphasis on written communications such as email	Yes	Yes	1–1.5 hours	X	X	X
10	Presentations		To provide insights into effective presentations and ideas to engage the customer more fully	Yes	Yes	1–1.25 hours	X	X	X

N = novice salespeople; E = experienced salespeople; M = sales management.

continued on next page

Table 1-1, continued

Sales Training Modules Matrix

CHAPTER	MODULE NAME	GAP ANALYSIS	OBJECTIVE	POWER-POINT SLIDES	ANCILLARY MATERIALS	DURATION OF SESSION	N	E	M
11	Features, Benefits, and Proof	Yes	To provide a simple method for creating and using benefit statements	Yes	Yes	45 minutes	X	X	X
12	Compelling Offers	Yes	To provide a method of collaborating with the customer to reach agreement	Yes	Yes	45–60 minutes	X	X	X
13	Networking	Yes	To provide skills for finding business in today's connected world	Yes	Yes	Less than 1 hour	X	X	X

N = novice salespeople; E = experienced salespeople; M = sales management.

Table 1–2

Half-Day Training Session for Novice Salespeople

TIME	MODULE/ACTIVITY	DURATION	WHERE TO FIND IN THE WORKBOOK
9:00 a.m.	Welcome and Check-in (introductions and expectations for the training)	15 minutes	Chapter 1, page 6
9:15 a.m.	Selling Today	30 minutes	Chapter 3, page 34
9:45 a.m.	Effective Selling	30 minutes	Chapter 3, page 38
10:15 a.m.	Break	15 minutes	
10:30 a.m.	Basic Knowledge	1.5 hours	Chapter 3, page 49
Noon	Check-out	15 minutes	Chapter 1, page 6

Table 1–3

Half-Day Training Session for Experienced Salespeople

TIME	MODULE/ACTIVITY	DURATION	WHERE TO FIND IN THE WORKBOOK
9:00 a.m.	Welcome and Check-in (introductions and expectations for the training)	15 minutes	Chapter 1, page 6
9:15 a.m.	Artful Listening	45 minutes	Chapter 8, page 132
10:00 a.m.	Break	15 minutes	
10:15 a.m.	Inquiry	1 hour	Chapter 8, page 137
11:15 a.m.	Break	15 minutes	
11:30 a.m.	Inquiry, continued	30 minutes	Chapter 8, page 137
Noon	Check-out	15 minutes	Chapter 1, page 6

SELF-STUDY OPTION

You can use a number of the modules as part of a self-study plan, including

◆ Basic Knowledge

◆ Planning and Organizing

◆ Communicating—A Basic Formula

◆ Presentations

◆ Features, Benefits, and Proof

◆ Compelling Offers.

Table 1–4

Full-Day Training Program A

TIME	MODULE/ACTIVITY	DURATION	WHERE TO FIND IN THE WORKBOOK
9:00 a.m.	Welcome and Check-in (introductions and expectations for the training)	15 minutes	Chapter 1, page 6
9:15 a.m.	Sales Mind Focus	1.25 hours	Chapter 4, page 77
10:30 a.m.	Break	15 minutes	
10:45 a.m.	Managing Tasks and Relationships	45 minutes	Chapter 5, page 91
11:30 a.m.	Break	15 minutes	
11:45 a.m.	Conditions of Satisfaction	45 minutes	Chapter 6, page 109
12:30 p.m.	Lunch	1.5 hours	
2:00 p.m.	Communicating—A Basic Formula	1 hour	Chapter 9, page 159
3:00 p.m.	Break	15 minutes	
3:15 p.m.	Communicating—A Basic Formula, continued	1.5 hours	Chapter 9, page 159
4:45 p.m.	Check-out	15 minutes	Chapter 1, page 6

Table 1–5

Full-Day Training Program B

TIME	MODULE/ACTIVITY	DURATION	WHERE TO FIND IN THE WORKBOOK
9:00 a.m.	Welcome and Check-in (introductions and expectations for the training)	15 minutes	Chapter 1, page 6
9:15 a.m.	Sales Mind Focus	1.25 hours	Chapter 4, page 77
10:30 a.m.	Break	15 minutes	
10:45 a.m.	Conditions of Satisfaction	45 minutes	Chapter 6, page 109
11:30 a.m.	Break	15 minutes	
11:45 a.m.	Features, Benefits, and Proof	45 minutes	Chapter 11, page 203
12:30 p.m.	Lunch	1.5 hours	
2:00 p.m.	Communicating—A Basic Formula	1 hour	Chapter 9, page 159
3:00 p.m.	Break	15 minutes	
3:15 p.m.	Communicating—A Basic Formula, continued	1.5 hours	Chapter 9, page 159
4:45 p.m.	Check-out	15 minutes	Chapter 1, page 6

Although individuals can tackle these modules themselves, interacting with a group adds richness and texture to the learner's experience that are unavailable in self-study. And shared learning experiences help build a culture of learning within an organization. One last word on self-study: make sure that individuals report in at least weekly on their progress and receive on-the-spot coaching and feedback. Without this the daily activities take over and the learning stops.

Icons

For easy reference, icons are included in the margins throughout this workbook to help you quickly locate key elements in training design and instruction. Here are the icons and what they represent:

Assessment: Appears when an agenda or learning activity includes an assessment and identifies each assessment presented.

CD: Indicates materials included on the CD accompanying this workbook.

Clock: Indicates suggested timeframes for an activity.

Discussion Question: Points out questions you can use to explore significant aspects of the training.

Key Point: Alerts you to key points that you should emphasize.

PowerPoint Slide: Indicates PowerPoint presentations and slides that you can use individually. Instructions for using PowerPoint slides and the CD are included in Appendix B.

Structured Exercise: Indicates group exercises that include some type of presentation to the class.

Tool: Identifies items that are helpful for the facilitator or the participants, before, during, or after the training session.

Training Instrument: Indicates interactive training activities.

What to Do Next: Denotes recommendations for what to do after completing a particular section of the workbook.

What's on the CD?

All the PowerPoint files, assessments, tools, and training instruments needed for each module are on the CD. In addition, there is a copy of Table 1–1: Sales Training Modules Matrix, which lists each module, its objective, the PowerPoint slides and ancillary materials needed, plus a recommendation for who would benefit from the module. This file will help you with your planning.

What to Do Next

* Study the entire contents of the book to get an overview of the resources it contains.

* Review the contents of the CD.

* Review the next chapter to make sure the terminology is consistent with your organization's terms and to help select attendees for the training.

◆ ◆ ◆

Now that you have a basic understanding of how this book is organized, you are ready to delve right into preparing for your training seminars. The next chapter will help you determine who will benefit from training and help you organize your training for those people.

Gap Analysis and Training Salespeople

What's in This Chapter?

- The three critical steps in adult learning

- A matrix that helps you determine who will benefit from training

- A tool to organize the learning process

- A series of useful tips for conducing sales training

What Is Learning?

Three critical steps in learning are

1. becoming aware of a gap—identifying what to learn

2. seeking understanding—taking a class, reading a book, getting a coach, and gaining the information needed to close the gap

3. undergoing transformation—putting learning into practice and making a commitment to overcome resistance to change.*

The first step in learning is to become aware that a gap exists in our knowledge or skills. Without this awareness it's impossible to seek out understanding. Sometimes awareness comes from external events, such as losing business or being told of a deficiency. Sometimes a person simply says, "I don't know how to do this."

For any salesperson, especially an experienced one, becoming aware of what he or she can do to improve may not come easily. To deal with such a situation, this book includes a gap analysis for 10 of the modules. The gap analysis will help novice salespeople track their learning after the training. At the

---

*Adapted from the work of Fred Kofman.

same time the gap analysis will help the experienced salesperson select the modules he or she needs to attend, and it can shed light on why the person's manager suggested he or she seek training.

You can use this book as part of your second step—prioritizing and planning actions for learning. Assessment 2–1: Sales Gap Analysis—Knowledge will help your sales personnel prioritize which topics to cover, and together with you and this book they can plan their learning activities. Here are the gap analysis assessments you will find at the end of this chapter and on the accompanying CD:

- ◆ Assessment 2–1: Sales Gap Analysis—Knowledge

- ◆ Assessment 2–2: Sales Gap Analysis—Sales Mind Focus

- ◆ Assessment 2–3: Sales Gap Analysis—Managing Tasks and Relationships

- ◆ Assessment 2–4: Sales Gap Analysis—Conditions of Satisfaction

- ◆ Assessment 2–5: Sales Gap Analysis—Listening, Inquiry, and Advocacy

- ◆ Assessment 2–6: Sales Gap Analysis—Communicating

- ◆ Assessment 2–7: Sales Gap Analysis—Benefits

- ◆ Assessment 2–8: Sales Gap Analysis—Networking.

In his book, *The Fifth Discipline: The Art and Practice of the Learning Organization*, Peter Senge talked about homeostasis—the tendency to maintain equilibrium or stability—and its affect on change or learning. He used the example of a thermostat to explain this natural phenomenon. When you set a thermostat to a particular temperature, it tells the heating and cooling system to turn on or off on the basis of a programmed setting. If you set the thermostat to 68 degrees when the room temperature is 70 degrees, the thermostat sends a signal to turn on the cooling system. Thus the thermostat keeps the temperature in a comfortable zone. As learners, we have a similar, natural desire to stay in a comfort zone or stick with what we know. It is almost biological and we often resist, even when we know change will help us. So we need support to integrate newly learned skills.

A follow-up system will help your sales personnel capture and use their learning. The system you develop should cover the third step of learning—supporting the learner to incorporate new habits. The commitment to learning can come only through an internal decision of the learner, which is related to the Willing and Able Matrix illustrated in Figure 2–1.

Who Should Be Trained?

The Willing and Able Matrix will help you and management direct training to those who will most benefit from it.

A person's manager should determine where that salesperson fits into the matrix. Therefore, you should use this matrix along with the gap analysis to review with managers the selection of salespeople to receive training.

Figure 2–1

Willing and Able Matrix

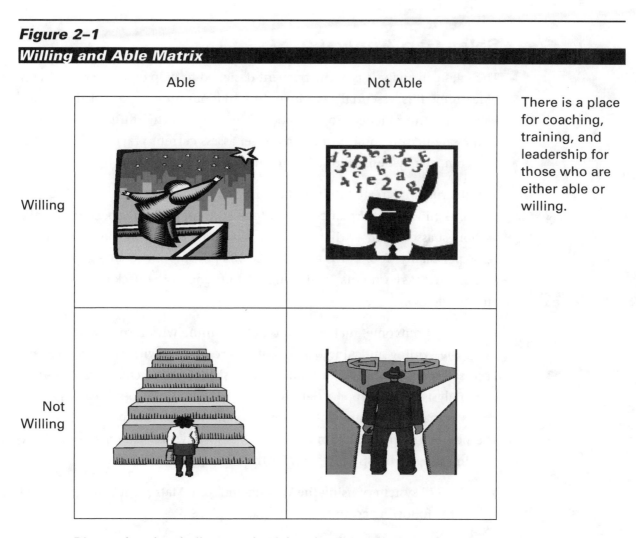

	Able	Not Able	
Willing			There is a place for coaching, training, and leadership for those who are either able or willing.
Not Willing			

Diagnosing the challenge + Applying the right solution = Success

Adapted with permission from *High Impact Training* by Todd Lapidus

Selection of willing and able and/or willing and not able sales personnel for training will provide you with the best opportunity to have learners in your sessions, instead of vacationers (able and not willing) or prisoners (not able and not willing). Having individuals who are able and not willing can lead to disruptive or apathetic behavior in the session. As for those who are not willing and not able, your training session will not save them and you should make management aware of this.

One last tip: training consumes many resources (for example, time away from the job, money for travel and the program, and the time and cost of the facilitator), so the best opportunity for return on investment is to train those who are willing.

Sales Gap Analysis

The sales gap analysis is an instrument designed to help organize the process of learning. It is, essentially, an inventory that outlines the knowledge, skills, behaviors, and practices in this book. The "gap" is the difference between how a salesperson and his or her manager assess current practices and the future competency desired for each line item and category.

This instrument, created to be self-administered, identifies the gaps that people think hinder performance. The intention is for each salesperson to make an honest assessment so that she or he can create a learning plan that makes sense personally. Tool 2–1 is an example of a portion of the sales gap analysis instruments (Assessments 2–1 through 2–8) found at the back of this chapter and on the CD.

For the best outcome, managers should determine whom they wish to train using the Willing and Able Matrix before proceeding with the gap analysis. Each salesperson who will attend training should complete the appropriate gap analysis for the appropriate module. You should also ask each participant's manager to complete the same gap analysis for that person. Then the salesperson and manager can review their respective assessments prior to the training to agree on specific goals for the training and follow-up.

This twofold system of using the Willing and Able Matrix with the gap analysis has the following advantages:

- ◆ You can prioritize training for each salesperson.

- ◆ You and the managers can identify where individuals fit on the Willing and Able Matrix.

Tool 2–1

Knowledge Gap Analysis

✔	KNOWLEDGE	1	2	3	4	5	6
	1. I have effective product/service knowledge so I can develop solutions/benefits for my customers.						
	2. I have effective competitor knowledge to offer implications and options to my customers so they can make informed decisions.						
	3. I have effective customer/market knowledge so that I do not waste my customer's time by asking questions for information that is readily available.						
	4. I have effective company knowledge so that I can represent our organization's values/mission and sell products at a profitable level.						

♦ You and the training participants have a clearer understanding of the managers' expectations.

♦ The salesperson and manager can use the gap analysis to track improvement after the training.

Tips for Training Salespeople

Salespeople are active; they want results fast; and when it comes to training, they want the answers to the challenges. That's the good news. The bad news is that these qualities can hinder adult learning. The biggest challenge in training salespeople is creating an active environment where they can make their own discoveries. To do this a person must reflect on what he or she does currently and how to improve. Many salespeople say in training, "tell me what works and I'll just do it." Salespeople view this as an efficient way to get immediate results. However, this does not happen most of the time because new tools often are difficult to use in the beginning. Frequently, people try new tools but discard them when they do not realize immediate results. And salespeople are too busy to take the time to modify or adapt tools to make them work.

By improving her or his skills through reflection and through approaching work from a disciplined perspective, a salesperson will become more innovative and more effective.

This book offers several methods to help salespeople keep active and explore their background for improvement. For new or inexperienced sales personnel, you must make a few modifications to the training; these modifications are noted in each chapter. In many sales training classes, you'll have a mixture of new and experienced salespeople. To assist you in that situation, this book is written in a sequence that a new salesperson would follow from cover to cover. Experienced salespeople should choose the modules that address their learning needs. Using the gap analysis to drive this training system allows you to execute a curriculum for both experienced and inexperienced salespeople. This motivates the veterans to learn and does not waste their time with material they already know.

Here are some general tips:

- Use real-life scenarios rather than hypothetical situations. Ask the salespeople to bring examples of their work. Case studies of actual situations are excellent tools.

- Most salespeople like to solve problems. Use this to your advantage by having small groups work on the answers that all salespeople want, such as how to create effective email messages, and then report to the full class. This is one way to get the salespeople to actively reflect and improve.

- Make sure you give them something they can use the day of or the day after the training. The gap analysis will help you identify what the salespeople want to learn.

- Use the term "practice" rather than "role-play." There often are negative connotations associated with role-plays because the participants can never exactly duplicate what happens with a customer. Practice implies that they are doing something to improve their skills, much like a sports team or a symphony does in scrimmages or rehearsals.

- For all-day sessions, allow long enough breaks during the day so the participants can answer email messages and check voice mail. Experienced salespeople get nervous when they are not in touch with their offices and customers. And no one wants to miss a sale!

- Set some simple rules for the training session, such as the following:

- ◆ Respect for time—be punctual.

- ◆ Respect for each other—keep private conversations to a minimum.

- ◆ Respect for the learning process—take a risk and try new skills; it's a safe place to practice.

◆ Take breaks every 55 to 70 minutes. Studies show that this is the limit for the human brain to focus and absorb.

◆ Engage everyone with an activity within the first 30 minutes. And plan an activity or exercise, even if it's short, during each hour of the training. Adults learn by doing!

What to Do Next

◆ Before using the sales gap analysis, read all of the modules in this book and become familiar with the skills used in the analysis. Then review the analysis to make sure the terminology and categories reflect your organization's cultural norms and terminology. If necessary, modify the language to align with your organization.

◆ Select the sales personnel to take the gap analysis (do this in conjunction with the managers responsible for the sales personnel). You can use the Willing and Able Matrix as part of the selection process. It is best to have sales personnel who will take training complete the gap analysis.

◆ Have the sales personnel and managers fill out the gap analysis. This can be assigned for individuals to complete on their own with a due date or you can hold a special meeting.

◆ After the sales personnel and managers have filled out the gap analysis, review the reports with the managers. If necessary, have the managers review the gap analysis with their sales personnel.

◆ Using the sales training matrix and the gap analysis, select the modules to be used for training. It is recommended that management be involved in the selection of modules.

◆ Use the training tips to help you plan and organize the training sessions.

◆◆◆

The first two chapters of this book outlined all the administrative tasks necessary to conduct successful sales training. Now you're ready to begin preparing your seminars. The next 11 chapters include the modules you will need for the sales training you will conduct. Although you can mix and match the modules as you see appropriate, they appear in a basic-to-advanced order. The next chapter addresses selling today, effective selling, sales cycles, and basic sales knowledge.

Assessment 2–1

Sales Gap Analysis—Knowledge

For: _____   Baseline Date: _____

Self-Assessment: Read each item under "Knowledge" in the chart below and mark an "A" in the column that reflects the knowledge and/or behavior you currently demonstrate.

Identify Goal: Review each item and mark a "B" in the column that is your goal for future competency. (*Note:* it is not necessary or practical to set goals for any category with a "6" rating.)

Gap: Now, draw a line between A and B on each item, illustrating the gap.

Action: Select the items that you would like to improve on and put a checkmark in the first column beside each choice. Write the bullet points of your learning plan in the space provided.

Going Forward: Check your progress monthly.

Rating Key:

1 = THIS IS NEW TO ME.

2 = I UNDERSTAND AND DEMONSTRATE THIS KNOWLEDGE/BEHAVIOR/SKILL LESS THAN 25 PERCENT OF THE TIME.

3 = I UNDERSTAND AND DEMONSTRATE THIS KNOWLEDGE/BEHAVIOR/SKILL 26–50 PERCENT OF THE TIME.

4 = I UNDERSTAND AND DEMONSTRATE THIS KNOWLEDGE/BEHAVIOR/SKILL 51–75 PERCENT OF THE TIME.

5 = I UNDERSTAND AND DEMONSTRATE THIS KNOWLEDGE/BEHAVIOR/SKILL 76 PERCENT OR MORE OF THE TIME.

6 = I USE THIS KNOWLEDGE/BEHAVIOR/SKILL TO ENHANCE CREATIVITY/ADAPTABILITY AND TO CREATE HIGHER STANDARDS.

✔	KNOWLEDGE	1	2	3	4	5	6
	1. I have effective product/service knowledge so I can develop solutions/benefits for my customers.						
	2. I have effective competitor knowledge to offer implications and options to my customers so they can make informed decisions.						
	3. I have effective customer/market knowledge so that I do not waste my customers' time by asking questions for information that is readily available.						
	4. I have effective company knowledge so that I can represent our organization's values/mission and sell products at a profitable level.						

Learning Plan:

Assessment 2–2

Sales Gap Analysis—Sales Mind Focus

For: _____ Baseline Date: _____

Self-Assessment: Read each item under "Sales Mind Focus" in the chart below and mark an "A" in the column that reflects the knowledge and/or behavior you currently demonstrate.

Identify Goal: Review each item and mark a "B" in the column that is your goal for future competency. (*Note:* it is not necessary or practical to set goals for any category with a "6" rating.)

Gap: Now, draw a line between A and B on each item, illustrating the gap.

Action: Select the items that you would like to improve on and put a checkmark in the first column beside each choice. Write the bullet points of your learning plan in the space provided.

Going Forward: Check your progress monthly.

Rating Key:

1 = THIS IS NEW TO ME.

2 = I UNDERSTAND AND DEMONSTRATE THIS KNOWLEDGE/BEHAVIOR/SKILL LESS THAN 25 PERCENT OF THE TIME.

3 = I UNDERSTAND AND DEMONSTRATE THIS KNOWLEDGE/BEHAVIOR/SKILL 26–50 PERCENT OF THE TIME.

4 = I UNDERSTAND AND DEMONSTRATE THIS KNOWLEDGE/BEHAVIOR/SKILL 51–75 PERCENT OF THE TIME.

5 = I UNDERSTAND AND DEMONSTRATE THIS KNOWLEDGE/BEHAVIOR/SKILL 76 PERCENT OR MORE OF THE TIME.

6 = I USE THIS KNOWLEDGE/BEHAVIOR/SKILL TO ENHANCE CREATIVITY/ADAPTABILITY AND TO CREATE HIGHER STANDARDS.

✓	SALES MIND FOCUS	1	2	3	4	5	6
	1. I separate fact from assumptions and opinions.						
	2. I review my assessments by rigorously analyzing data, assumptions, and concerns for the purpose of taking effective action.						
	3. Using sales mind focus thinking skills, I develop effective strategies for my accounts.						
	4. Using strategic thinking skills, I prepare for all of my interactions with customers.						

Learning Plan:

Assessment 2–3

Sales Gap Analysis—Managing Tasks and Relationships

For: _____ Baseline Date: _____

Self-Assessment: Read each item under "Managing Tasks and Relationships" in the chart below and mark an "A" in the column that reflects the knowledge and/or behavior you currently demonstrate.

Identify Goal: Review each item and mark a "B" in the column that is your goal for future competency. (*Note:* it is not necessary or practical to set goals for any category with a "6" rating.)

Gap: Now, draw a line between A and B on each item, illustrating the gap.

Action: Select the items that you would like to improve on and put a checkmark in the first column beside each choice. Write the bullet points of your learning plan in the space provided.

Going Forward: Check your progress monthly.

Rating Key:

1 = THIS IS NEW TO ME.

2 = I UNDERSTAND AND DEMONSTRATE THIS KNOWLEDGE/BEHAVIOR/SKILL LESS THAN 25 PERCENT OF THE TIME.

3 = I UNDERSTAND AND DEMONSTRATE THIS KNOWLEDGE/BEHAVIOR/SKILL 26–50 PERCENT OF THE TIME.

4 = I UNDERSTAND AND DEMONSTRATE THIS KNOWLEDGE/BEHAVIOR/SKILL 51–75 PERCENT OF THE TIME.

5 = I UNDERSTAND AND DEMONSTRATE THIS KNOWLEDGE/BEHAVIOR/SKILL 76 PERCENT OR MORE OF THE TIME.

6 = I USE THIS KNOWLEDGE/BEHAVIOR/SKILL TO ENHANCE CREATIVITY/ADAPTABILITY AND TO CREATE HIGHER STANDARDS.

✓	MANAGING TASKS AND RELATIONSHIPS	1	2	3	4	5	6
	1. I make sure my activities support the tasks and relationships appropriate for each of my accounts.						
	2. I regularly assess my relationships with my accounts so that I minimize time spent repairing relationships.						
	3. I align my style and my offer to each customer's style and situation.						
	4. I regularly show appreciation to my customers beyond the sale or task.						

Learning Plan:

Assessment 2–4

Sales Gap Analysis—Conditions of Satisfaction

For: _____   Baseline Date: _____

Self-Assessment: Read each item under "Conditions of Satisfaction" in the chart below and mark an "A" in the column that reflects the knowledge and/or behavior you currently demonstrate.

Identify Goal: Review each item and mark a "B" in the column that is your goal for future competency. (*Note:* it is not necessary or practical to set goals for any category with a "6" rating.)

Gap: Now, draw a line between A and B on each item, illustrating the gap.

Action: Select the items that you would like to improve on and put a checkmark in the first column beside each choice. Write the bullet points of your learning plan in the space provided.

Going Forward: Check your progress monthly.

Rating Key:

1 = THIS IS NEW TO ME.

2 = I UNDERSTAND AND DEMONSTRATE THIS KNOWLEDGE/BEHAVIOR/SKILL LESS THAN 25 PERCENT OF THE TIME.

3 = I UNDERSTAND AND DEMONSTRATE THIS KNOWLEDGE/BEHAVIOR/SKILL 26–50 PERCENT OF THE TIME.

4 = I UNDERSTAND AND DEMONSTRATE THIS KNOWLEDGE/BEHAVIOR/SKILL 51–75 PERCENT OF THE TIME.

5 = I UNDERSTAND AND DEMONSTRATE THIS KNOWLEDGE/BEHAVIOR/SKILL 76 PERCENT OR MORE OF THE TIME.

6 = I USE THIS KNOWLEDGE/BEHAVIOR/SKILL TO ENHANCE CREATIVITY/ADAPTABILITY AND TO CREATE HIGHER STANDARDS.

✓	CONDITIONS OF SATISFACTION	1	2	3	4	5	6
	1. I clearly define and capture explicit conditions of satisfaction.						
	2. I uncover implicit conditions of satisfaction.						
	3. I verify conditions of satisfaction with my customers.						
	4. I use conditions of satisfaction to drive my offers.						

Learning Plan:

Assessment 2–5

Sales Gap Analysis—Listening, Inquiry, and Advocacy

For: _____   Baseline Date: _____

Self-Assessment: Read each item under "Listening, Inquiry, and Advocacy" in the chart below and mark an "A" in the column that reflects the knowledge and/or behavior you currently demonstrate.

Identify Goal: Review each item and mark a "B" in the column that is your goal for future competency. (*Note:* it is not necessary or practical to set goals for any category with a "6" rating.)

Gap: Now, draw a line between A and B on each item, illustrating the gap.

Action: Select the items that you would like to improve on and put a checkmark in the first column beside each choice. Write the bullet points of your learning plan in the space provided.

Going Forward: Check your progress monthly.

Rating Key:

1 = THIS IS NEW TO ME.

2 = I UNDERSTAND AND DEMONSTRATE THIS KNOWLEDGE/BEHAVIOR/SKILL LESS THAN 25 PERCENT OF THE TIME.

3 = I UNDERSTAND AND DEMONSTRATE THIS KNOWLEDGE/BEHAVIOR/SKILL 26–50 PERCENT OF THE TIME.

4 = I UNDERSTAND AND DEMONSTRATE THIS KNOWLEDGE/BEHAVIOR/SKILL 51–75 PERCENT OF THE TIME.

5 = I UNDERSTAND AND DEMONSTRATE THIS KNOWLEDGE/BEHAVIOR/SKILL 76 PERCENT OR MORE OF THE TIME.

6 = I USE THIS KNOWLEDGE/BEHAVIOR/SKILL TO ENHANCE CREATIVITY/ADAPTABILITY AND TO CREATE HIGHER STANDARDS.

✓	LISTENING, INQUIRY, AND ADVOCACY	1	2	3	4	5	6
	1. I use effective questions to uncover and understand my customers' conditions of satisfaction, concerns, needs, and motivation.						
	2. I craft questions that evoke comfortable disclosure of facts and feelings.						
	3. I frame linking questions that deepen dialogue.						
	4. I listen with empathy for unspoken concerns and implicit conditions of satisfaction.						
	5. I clarify word traps and other potential misconceptions to help stay in alignment with my customers.						
	6. I advocate my opinions in alignment with my customers' concerns and conditions of satisfaction.						

Learning Plan:

Assessment 2–6
Sales Gap Analysis—Communicating

For: _____ Baseline Date: _____

Self-Assessment: Read each item under "Communicating" in the chart below and mark an "A" in the column that reflects the knowledge and/or behavior you currently demonstrate.

Identify Goal: Review each item and mark a "B" in the column that is your goal for future competency. (*Note:* it is not necessary or practical to set goals for any category with a "6" rating.)

Gap: Now, draw a line between A and B on each item, illustrating the gap.

Action: Select the items that you would like to improve on and put a checkmark in the first column beside each choice. Write the bullet points of your learning plan in the space provided.

Going Forward: Check your progress monthly.

Rating Key:

1 = THIS IS NEW TO ME.

2 = I UNDERSTAND AND DEMONSTRATE THIS KNOWLEDGE/BEHAVIOR/SKILL LESS THAN 25 PERCENT OF THE TIME.

3 = I UNDERSTAND AND DEMONSTRATE THIS KNOWLEDGE/BEHAVIOR/SKILL 26–50 PERCENT OF THE TIME.

4 = I UNDERSTAND AND DEMONSTRATE THIS KNOWLEDGE/BEHAVIOR/SKILL 51–75 PERCENT OF THE TIME.

5 = I UNDERSTAND AND DEMONSTRATE THIS KNOWLEDGE/BEHAVIOR/SKILL 76 PERCENT OR MORE OF THE TIME.

6 = I USE THIS KNOWLEDGE/BEHAVIOR/SKILL TO ENHANCE CREATIVITY/ADAPTABILITY AND TO CREATE HIGHER STANDARDS.

✓	COMMUNICATING	1	2	3	4	5	6
	1. I craft messages that add value for my customers and conform to my company's brand and style.						
	2. I customize my communication with consideration of my customers' style and our relationship.						
	3. I actively practice the use of professional, positive, and authentic language.						
	4. I am disciplined in my approach to proofreading and dispatching communications.						
	5. My communications are focused on my customer.						

Learning Plan:

Assessment 2–7
Sales Gap Analysis—Benefits

For: _____ Baseline Date: _____

Self-Assessment: Read each item under "Benefits" in the chart below and mark an "A" in the column that reflects the knowledge and/or behavior you currently demonstrate.

Identify Goal: Review each item and mark a "B" in the column that is your goal for future competency. (*Note:* it is not necessary or practical to set goals for any category with a "6" rating.)

Gap: Now, draw a line between A and B on each item, illustrating the gap.

Action: Select the items that you would like to improve on and put a checkmark in the first column beside each choice. Write the bullet points of your learning plan in the space provided.

Going Forward: Check your progress monthly.

Rating Key:

1 = THIS IS NEW TO ME.

2 = I UNDERSTAND AND DEMONSTRATE THIS KNOWLEDGE/BEHAVIOR/SKILL LESS THAN 25 PERCENT OF THE TIME.

3 = I UNDERSTAND AND DEMONSTRATE THIS KNOWLEDGE/BEHAVIOR/SKILL 26–50 PERCENT OF THE TIME.

4 = I UNDERSTAND AND DEMONSTRATE THIS KNOWLEDGE/BEHAVIOR/SKILL 51–75 PERCENT OF THE TIME.

5 = I UNDERSTAND AND DEMONSTRATE THIS KNOWLEDGE/BEHAVIOR/SKILL 76 PERCENT OR MORE OF THE TIME.

6 = I USE THIS KNOWLEDGE/BEHAVIOR/SKILL TO ENHANCE CREATIVITY/ADAPTABILITY AND TO CREATE HIGHER STANDARDS.

✓	BENEFITS	1	2	3	4	5	6
	1. I develop and update a repertoire of refined benefit statements that are easily customized.						
	2. My benefit statements are customized and create impact.						
	3. I link benefits to my customers' explicit and implicit conditions of satisfaction.						
	4. I quantify the impact of the benefits and solutions that I offer.						
	5. I use credible proof.						

Learning Plan:

Assessment 2–8
Sales Gap Analysis—Networking

For: _____ Baseline Date: _____

Self-Assessment: Read each item under "Networking" in the chart below and mark an "A" in the column that reflects the knowledge and/or behavior you currently demonstrate.

Identify Goal: Review each item and mark a "B" in the column that is your goal for future competency. (*Note:* it is not necessary or practical to set goals for any category with a "6" rating.)

Gap: Now, draw a line between A and B on each item, illustrating the gap.

Action: Select the items that you would like to improve on and put a checkmark in the first column beside each choice. Write the bullet points of your learning plan in the space provided.

Going Forward: Check your progress monthly.

Rating Key:

1 = THIS IS NEW TO ME.

2 = I UNDERSTAND AND DEMONSTRATE THIS KNOWLEDGE/BEHAVIOR/SKILL LESS THAN 25 PERCENT OF THE TIME.

3 = I UNDERSTAND AND DEMONSTRATE THIS KNOWLEDGE/BEHAVIOR/SKILL 26–50 PERCENT OF THE TIME.

4 = I UNDERSTAND AND DEMONSTRATE THIS KNOWLEDGE/BEHAVIOR/SKILL 51–75 PERCENT OF THE TIME.

5 = I UNDERSTAND AND DEMONSTRATE THIS KNOWLEDGE/BEHAVIOR/SKILL 76 PERCENT OR MORE OF THE TIME.

6 = I USE THIS KNOWLEDGE/BEHAVIOR/SKILL TO ENHANCE CREATIVITY/ADAPTABILITY AND TO CREATE HIGHER STANDARDS.

✓	NETWORKING	1	2	3	4	5	6
	1. I create and evolve a networking strategy.						
	2. I devote adequate time and energy to cultivating my network.						
	3. I find creative ways to disperse value to my network.						
	4. I am involved in community activities and community building.						

Learning Plan:

The Building Blocks of Effective Sales Personnel

What's in This Chapter?

- An explanation of the value-added approach to selling

- A comprehensive list of key points to effective selling

- Four sales training modules that address aspects of success: selling today, effective selling, sales cycles, and basic knowledge

- A detailed program agenda for each module

We live in a world of oversupply, and selling is very different from what it was even a few years ago. Buyers have experienced a dramatic increase in the variety of choices and information available to them, something that has fundamentally shifted the tone and pace of sales relationships.

Most sales techniques are based on scarcity: scarcity of appropriate choices and scarcity of information about what is available. This has led to the development of manipulative sales techniques that focus on playing the numbers. Make x number of calls and send x number of proposals, you'll close x number of sales and send x number of clients to the dead file.

The world of oversupply has eroded the effectiveness of this type of sales mindset and brought to light the need for value-added approaches. A salesperson can add value by focusing on relationship building and helping the customer evaluate the best options from the huge array of available choices. This approach aligns with the way many customers expect to be treated by a professional salesperson.

An approach that seeks to add value requires a thorough understanding of how the customer defines value. A transactional approach is manipulative and focused on making a sale. Instead, a customer-centered approach adds value.

Key Points to Effective Selling

- ◆ Oversupply of choice and information has significantly changed the salesperson's role.

- ◆ It is important for salespeople to understand that customers have more choices and more control over their choices. This requires a value-added approach as opposed to a transactional approach.

- ◆ With more information and choices, customers have become more demanding.

- ◆ The customer wants added value from sales personnel in the sales process.

CD Resources

Materials for the modules in this chapter appear in this workbook and as electronic files on the accompanying CD. Insert the CD and open the "PDF Files" folder to locate electronic copies of the training instruments and tools mentioned in this chapter. The PowerPoint presentations are also on the CD. You will find more detailed instructions and help in locating files on the CD by referring to Appendix C, "Using the Compact Disc," at the back of the workbook.

Selling Today Module

This is an introductory module that can be used with any type of group (a mix of experienced and new salespeople or separate groups of experienced and new salespeople).

You can use this module to start any sales training program because it quickly engages the participants and provides you with information to link with key points brought forward in the other training modules.

TRAINING OBJECTIVE

The primary objective of this module is to make your sales personnel aware that their customers have more choices than ever before and more information about their choices. In this environment salespeople have to add value in the sales process or the customer either will go elsewhere or will use price as the primary reason for purchasing.

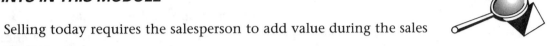

KEY POINTS IN THIS MODULE

- ◆ Selling today requires the salesperson to add value during the sales process.

- ◆ Customers have more choices and more information about those choices.

MATERIALS

- ◆ Two flipchart easels with paper and colored markers

- ◆ LCD projector, screen, and computer for running the PowerPoint presentation

- ◆ PowerPoint slides 3–1 through 3–5. Copies of the slides for this module, *Selling Today.ppt,* are included at the end of this chapter.

SAMPLE AGENDA

9:00 a.m.   Show slide 3–1. Tell the participants that film actor and director Woody Allen, while making fun of the stereotype held about many salespeople, has made a point about the manipulative practices of selling, which no longer apply.

Table 3–1
Slide Information for the Selling Today Module

NUMBER	TITLE/TOPIC	DESCRIPTION	TIME
3–1	Title slide: Selling today	Provides the opportunity for the class to get settled and the facilitator to welcome the group as appropriate	2 minutes
3–2	World of oversupply	Customers have more choices and more information about their choices. Customers want sales people to add value. Discussion question	2 minutes
3–3	Adding value	Structured exercise	10 minutes
3–4	Customer focus and you	Discussion question	5 minutes
3–5	End of the module		

9:05 Show slide 3–2. Tell the participants that we live in a world of oversupply and selling has changed. There has been a dramatic increase in the variety of choices available to customers. This oversupply of choice and information has shifted the tone and pace of sales relationships. You can add value by focusing on relationship building and becoming more of an adviser or decision facilitator. This is how customers expect to be treated by professional salespeople.

Introduce the following discussion question: *What are the choices that your customers have?*

Note: In addition to the obvious choices a customer has, such as a competitor's product, you want the group to come up with some answers that might not be so obvious. For example:

◆ For discretionary purchases, the choices that a customer has are more than just the product you are selling. A home theater system might be competing with a new deck for the house or a vacation.

◆ A new software program might be competing with a new piece of machinery on the priority list for capital expenditures.

◆ New office furniture might be competing with a new telephone system.

Ask the following discussion question: *What information is available to your customers about their choices?*

Possible answers include these:

◆ what salespeople can tell them

◆ what they can learn via the Internet

◆ information available from consumer organizations, magazines, newspapers, colleagues, and friends.

Ask the following discussion question: *What do you think are the possible results to an oversupply of choice and information?*

9:15   Show slide 3–3. Say to the participants that the world of oversupply has eroded the effectiveness of the conventional sales mindset and brought to light the need for value-added approaches. You can add value by focusing on relationship building and helping the customer evaluate the best options from the supply of available choices. This approach aligns with the way most customers expect to be treated by a professional salesperson.

Structured Exercise 3–1

This is an idea-generation exercise for the class, conducted in small groups.

Step 1: Split the class into pairs or groups of three to five people.

Step 2: Ask them to come up with ideas that would add value for their customers in the sales process. Remind them that this exercise is about how *they* add value, not how a product or service adds value. Give them 10–15 minutes to come up with their ideas.

Step 3: Have each group select a spokesperson to share the ideas with the class. As the ideas are shared, write them on a flipchart. Possible ideas that the groups think of might include the following:

   ◆   Find out as much as possible about the customer before we meet so that we don't waste his or her time with questions other salespeople have asked.

   ◆   Be respectful of the customer's time.

   ◆   Present the right product/service/solution and don't oversell.

9:30   Show slide 3–4. Introduce the following discussion question: *As a professional salesperson, what are the metrics that you use to know whether customers think you add value for them?*

Here you are looking for participants' understanding that their primary function is to sell and generate revenue for the organization. Therefore it is important to be aware of activities, ratios, and numbers to make sure the salesforce is being productive with their efforts. The salesperson selling today has to be productive and satisfy her or his customers. Each action is of equal importance and one does not exist without the other.

9:45   Show slide 3–5. This is the end of the module.

Effective Selling Module

TRAINING OBJECTIVE

The primary objective of this module is to provide the participants an overview of and an orientation to effective selling. This module is designed to get your group talking about what knowledge and abilities an effective salesperson possesses in four areas:

1. matching customers to products/services/solutions

2. communicating effectively

3. thinking strategically

4. building effective relationships.

These four topics make up all the activities a salesperson engages in with her or his customers. On the surface each of these topics seems to describe straightforward activities of salespeople. However, to repeat an often-used phrase, "easy to say and hard to do" is probably more accurate in describing these activities. What knowledge and what abilities are needed for these activities? This book certainly offers some answers, but the more important answers might lie in the thoughts and opinions of your sales personnel. Combining what they know with the content of this book can be very powerful.

KEY POINTS IN THIS MODULE

◆ There are no right or wrong answers to the exercises in this module.

◆ This module is about getting participants to share their thoughts, opinions, and ideas. Combining participants' ideas and insights with the content in this book can be very powerful.

◆ This is an introductory module that can be used with any type of group (a mix of experienced and new salespeople or separate groups of experienced and new salespeople).

MATERIALS

◆ Two flipchart easels with paper and colored markers

◆ LCD projector, screen, and computer for running the PowerPoint presentation

◆ PowerPoint slides 3–6 through 3–12. (Copies of the slides for this module, *Effective Selling.ppt,* are included at the end of this chapter.)

SAMPLE AGENDA

9:00 a.m.   Show slide 3–6. Tell the participants that selling is about doing, not trying. The quote from Yoda is from the movie *The Empire Strikes Back.* The scene has Luke Skywalker doing a one-handed handstand with Yoda standing on one of his feet while using "the force" to lift his cross-wing fighter out of the swamp. Just when Luke gets the fighter out of the swamp, he loses concentration and the fighter falls back, Luke collapses, and Yoda falls to the ground. Yoda dusts off and says, in a frustrated voice, "What happened?" Luke answers in an exasperated tone, "I tried, Master." At this point Yoda responds, "Do or not do—there is no try." Trying at sales is unproductive; doing one's best leads to learning and improving, which results in more sales.

9:05   Show slide 3–7. Tell the participants that to match the right product/service/solution to the right customer at the right price they need to

◆ communicate effectively

◆ think and act strategically

◆ proactively build the right-size relationship.

9:10   Show slide 3–8. Ask the participants the following question: *What are the attributes and activities associated with matching the right product/service/solution to the right cus-*

tomer at the right price? Introduce Structured Exercise 3–2. It is designed to get the participants thinking and talking about an important aspect of selling that is rarely explored in the hectic pace of the workplace. Tell the participants that you are not looking for the right answers— you are looking to uncover the collective wisdom of the group so that everyone can learn from each other.

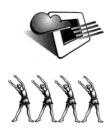

Now show slide 3–9.

Structured Exercise 3–2

Step 1: Split the class into pairs or groups of three to five people and ask them to answer the question you posed above.

Step 2: Give them five to eight minutes and have a spokesperson from each group share the ideas generated.

Step 3: Write the ideas on a flipchart.

Structured Exercise 3–3

Step 1: Split the class into pairs or groups of three to five people and have them answer the following question: *What are the attributes and activities associated with communicating effectively?*

Step 2: Give them five to eight minutes and have a spokesperson from each group share the ideas generated.

Step 3: Write the ideas on a flipchart.

9:15   Show slide 3–10. Ask the participants the following question: *What are the attributes and activities associated with thinking and acting strategically?* The following exercise continues the thinking started in the previous exercise. Explain again that you are seeking the collective wisdom or implicit knowledge of the class.

Table 3–2

Slide Information for the Effective Selling Module

NUMBER	TITLE/TOPIC	DESCRIPTION	TIME
3–6	Title slide: Effective selling	Provides the opportunity for the class to get settled and the facilitator to welcome the group as appropriate	2–5 minutes
3–7	A salesperson has the knowledge or ability	Three key activities a salesperson performs to be successful	1 minute
3–8	Matching the right product/service to the right customer at the right price	Structured exercise	5–10 minutes
3–9	Communicating effectively	Structured exercise	5–10 minutes
3–10	Thinking and acting strategically	Structured exercise	5–10 minutes
3–11	Building effective relationships	Structured exercise	5–10 minutes
3–12	End of the module		

Structured Exercise 3–4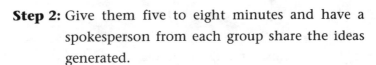

Step 1: Split the class into pairs or groups of three to five people and have them answer the question you posed above.

Step 2: Give them five to eight minutes and have a spokesperson from each group share the ideas generated.

Step 3: Write the ideas on a flipchart.

9:25   Show slide 3–11. Ask the participants the following question: *What are the attributes and activities associated with building an effective relationship with a customer?* This exercise again continues the thinking exercises. It might be good at this point to put the participants into different groups.

Structured Exercise 3–5

Step 1: Split the class into pairs or groups of three to five people and have them answer the above question.

Step 2: Give them five to eight minutes and have a spokesperson from each pair or group share the ideas generated.

Step 3: Write the ideas on a flipchart and save for future use in other training modules.

9:35   Show slide 3–12. To finish this module you can review the flipcharts with all the ideas the participants developed or you can ask for volunteers to share what new ideas they have learned. Then review the key points of effective selling and ask the participants to "do or not do—there is no try."

Sales Cycles Module

A sales cycle is part of a business process. In most cases the process starts with some type of sales cycle that can be as short as a minute (selling a hamburger in a fast-food restaurant) or can last for years (selling an electric generator to a utility company). Effective sales personnel understand their sales cycle and its role within their organization's business process.

Sales cycles come in many forms and descriptions. They all essentially span the time and process from when the salesperson and the customer decide to do business together through the delivery of the product or service. These activities can include researching the customer, phone calls, in-person sales calls, proposals, sending the account to an inactive file, putting a task force together to create new solutions for the customer, and so forth. Depending on your business, each activity or section of the sales cycle carries different importance. For inside-sales positions where the sales cycle is short, the preparation stage might be the most important because the amount of time spent with a customer is brief. The salesperson needs to be well prepared with product knowledge (features and benefits), competitor knowledge, customer knowledge, proper use of collateral, and an understanding of how to use the sales administration system so that follow-up is fast and effective. When the sales cycle is longer and there is more interaction between the salesperson and a client, managing the cycle becomes more important so that the salesperson is using his or her time effectively.

A defined sales cycle or process is an important tool to help salespeople stay organized and on track. The sales cycle helps salespeople prioritize their time. By knowing how many accounts or customers they are working with and where each account or customer is in the sales cycle, they will know where to spend their time. Here's an example: A salesperson has the majority of his or her accounts well along in the sales cycle and only a few accounts at the beginning of the cycle. If no action is taken to secure new prospects, this salesperson will find himself or herself with a sales drought.

A defined sales process also helps sales managers have conversations with their salespeople about where they are with each client. This understanding helps the sales manager predict how much more time or effort might be needed to make the sale, or it may tell the manager that the salesperson is spending too much time with a client.

TRAINING OBJECTIVE

The objective of this module is to provide an overview of basic sales cycles and the organization's specific sales cycle.

KEY POINTS IN THIS MODULE

- ◆ Sales cycles are an important tool for the salesperson and his or her manager.

- ◆ Effective sales personnel understand their sales cycle and its role within their organization's business process.

- ◆ Each activity or phase of the sales cycle occurs in a sequence with the purpose of guiding the customer to a decision.

- ◆ An organized approach to using a sales cycle results in more business.

This module can be used for the following reasons:

- ◆ You have inexperienced salespeople and you want to give them an overview of sale cycles.

- ◆ You want your sales personnel to think about and identify the activities within your organization's sales cycle.

◆ There is no defined sales cycle or process for your organization, and you wish to use this module as a start for determining a sales cycle.

MATERIALS

◆ Two flipchart easels with paper and colored markers

◆ LCD projector, screen, and computer for running the PowerPoint presentation

◆ PowerPoint slides 3–13 through 3–18. (Copies of the slides for this module, *Sales Cycles.ppt,* are included at the end of this chapter.)

SAMPLE AGENDA

9:00 a.m. Show slide 3–13. Share with the participants that selling follows a common-sense cycle, as this often-used quote depicts. Obviously you do not present a contract to a customer you are speaking to for the first time, but salespeople often send a proposal before the client is ready (also known as a "premature proposal").

Table 3–3

Slide Information for the Sales Cycles Module

NUMBER	TITLE/TOPIC	DESCRIPTION	TIME
3–13	Title slide: Sales cycles	Provides the opportunity for the class to get settled and the facilitator to welcome the group as appropriate	1 minute
3–14	Workflow	Illustration of the workflow of a business that includes the sales process, delivery, and customer satisfaction	5–8 minutes
3–15	Different sales cycles	Different versions of sales cycles	1 minute
3–16	Sales process	Example of a sales process	3–5 minutes
3–17	What works for you?	Structured exercise	15–20 minutes
3–18	End of the module		

9:05   Show slide 3–14. Say that this model, developed by Fernando Flores, represents the essence of a business process. Then go over the sections of the workflow model:

Preparation: The business prepares itself to offer products, and the salesforce gets ready to contact customers. The result is that the customers either make a request for the product/service or consider purchasing a product or service.

Assessment and Negotiation: The salesperson and the customer are assessing each other. The customer is determining if the product is right for him or her, and the salesperson is making assessments about the chances of getting the customer to purchase. The outcome of this stage is, hopefully, an agreement.

Performance: This stage is the delivery of the product or service by the organization, based on the agreement reached between the customer and salesperson. At the completion of the performance, the organization declares that it has completed the conditions in the agreement.

Acceptance: After the declaration of completion, the customer determines whether she or he is satisfied.

9:15   Show slide 3–15. Note the three cycles for the audience (funnel, continuum, and phase). Tell your participants that there are many different sales cycles and ways to describe them. Some use metaphors, such as the funnel or farming (tilling the soil, planting the seed, watering and fertilizing, and then harvesting).

The funnel shows that there are many prospects, and as prospects continue down the funnel many drop out for various reasons, leading to the customers who decide to buy. The funnel metaphor implies that the number of sales is a percentage of the number of prospects a salesperson starts with, and thus the more prospects, the more chance of increased sales.

The continuum represents the repetitive nature of sales. You work with a customer until a sale is made, or not, and then move on to the next customer.

The phased sales cycle is about completing one phase before moving to the next; this is more of a sequential model.

All sales cycles are more similar than they are different, and there really is no right cycle other than the one that makes sense for your organization.

9:20

Show slide 3–16. Say that this is a simplified flowchart to show an example of a sales process for a phased sales cycle. Go over the model this way:

Phase I (the discovery phase) is complete when the salesperson has determined that the customer has the interest and the ability to purchase and use the product/service. Although the salesperson decides the next steps, the decision to move to Phase II belongs to the customer.

Phase II (the customer consideration and decision stage) is complete when the customer decides to purchase or not. If the customer decides not to purchase, the salesperson may have to return to an early part of Phase II or even Phase I.

Phase III (the purchase stage) is when a salesperson sends out a contract. If the client does not accept the contract, the salesperson returns to Phase II activities to uncover more conditions of satisfaction, if any.

Phase IV (the customer receipt and use stage) is when the operations unit of the organization takes over the relationship with the customer. Many organizations build in a step to foster feedback of customer satisfaction information to the salesperson so he or she can follow up for future business.

9:25

Show slide 3–17. Introduce the structured exercise. Explain that this exercise is intended to make participants think about and identify what happens in the sales cycle for your organization. It is by reviewing the activities that we can discover where we might be putting the cart before the horse.

Structured Exercise 3–6

Step 1: Split the class into groups of three to five people and have them answer these five questions:

1. What activities take place in the sales cycle?

2. What is the order of activities?

3. How much time does the cycle take and how much time is needed for each step?

4. Why is understanding your sales cycle important?

5. For your product/service, which part of the sales cycle is most important, and why?

Step 2: In addition to answering the questions, have each group draw a sales cycle or sales process (provide two to three pieces of flipchart paper and markers).

Step 3: Give 15–20 minutes and then have each group select a spokesperson to share the group's answers and sales cycle or process.

Step 4: Write the ideas on a flipchart and save for future use in other training modules.

Note to facilitator: You can modify the questions and eliminate any that are not applicable to your situation. For example, you might want to focus on activities and the order of activities if the sales personnel are not spending enough time qualifying accounts or are asking for the business too early.

Here are responses to the questions:

◆ *What activities take place in the sales cycle?*

 ◆ research and qualification

 ◆ sales calls (phone or in person)

 ◆ correspondence

 ◆ paperwork

 ◆ proposals and contracts.

◆ *What is the order of activities?*

 ◆ Each organization is a little different. The key points to uncover are that the order of activities must make sense to the customer and that the salesperson is not asking for the business too soon. To use some sales jargon, avoid premature proposals. When this happens the customer is not ready for a proposal and might assume that the salesperson didn't listen or understand him or her—even worse, the customer feels pressure to purchase.

◆ *How much time does the cycle take, and how much time is needed for each step?*

 ◆ Again, each organization is a little different. Make sure your salespeople are realistic about the time needed for each step. To do this you can ask them to explain their thinking and what experience/data/facts they have to support it.

◆ *Why is knowing your sales cycle important?*

 ◆ helps me keep track of my productivity

 ◆ helps me match the customer's pace

 ◆ helps me to focus on new business so I keep my pipeline full

 ◆ helps me plan my day and prepare for sales calls

 ◆ helps me get more business.

◆ *For your product/service, which part of the sales cycle is most important, and why?*

    ◆ Look for responses that draw a correlation to time in the sales cycle. All parts of the cycle are important, but the objective is to make the sale. The importance of this question is that salespeople are spending time purposefully, which leads to the sale in each stage of the cycle.

9:45   Show slide 3–18. The simplest and possibly most effective way to end the module is to ask each participant to share what she or he has learned from the module.

Basic Knowledge Module

The famous football coach Vince Lombardi used to start his football camps by holding a football and stating, "Gentlemen, this is a football." This was his reminder that without basic knowledge the team could not achieve its goals.

The same is true for salespeople. Before a salesperson can interact effectively with customers, he or she needs to have basic knowledge of the product/service, competitors, and customers. Imagine trying to convince a customer to buy from you when you cannot answer questions about your product—how embarrassing! Also, not being aware of a competitor can blindside a salesperson.

Today, customer knowledge is even more important than product knowledge. If a salesperson does not do her or his homework about a customer, many negative consequences will occur. Customers do not have the time or inclination to educate the suppliers about their business—they expect their suppliers to be informed.

This module, which actually comprises three mini-modules, can either provide a starting point for basic knowledge training or supplement your existing training for product/service, competitor, and customer knowledge. You can present each mini-module separately. For example, if your salespeople have effective knowledge of products or competitors but need to improve their customer knowledge, you may offer just a session on customer knowledge. You can easily modify the worksheets and examples for these mini-modules, depending on your situation.

TRAINING OBJECTIVE

The objective of this module is to provide the basic knowledge needed before a salesperson can effectively present products and services and interact with customers.

KEY POINTS IN THIS MODULE

◆ Knowing your product, competitors, and customers is basic to being an effective salesperson.

◆ Customers are more knowledgeable and less patient then ever before. Don't waste their time asking for information that you can obtain on your own.

◆ Customers who know that the salesperson does not know much about them or their organization have an advantage, especially in price negotiations.

MATERIALS

◆ Two flipchart easels with paper and colored markers

◆ Training Instrument 3–1: Product Knowledge Worksheet

◆ Tool 3–1: Worksheet Example A: Product Knowledge

◆ Tool 3–2: Worksheet Example B: Product Knowledge

◆ Training Instrument 3–2: Competitor Knowledge Worksheet

◆ Tool 3–3: Worksheet Example: Competitor Knowledge

◆ Training Instrument 3–3: Top Competitors Summary Worksheet

◆ Tool 3–4: Worksheet Example: Top Competitor Summary

◆ Training Instrument 3–4: Individual and Corporate Customer Knowledge Worksheet

◆ Tool 3–5: Worksheet Example: Individual and Corporate Customer Knowledge

Note: This module does not use a PowerPoint presentation.

TIMING FOR MINI-MODULES

- ◆ Product Knowledge: 15–20 minutes

- ◆ Competitor Knowledge: 20–30 minutes

- ◆ Customer Knowledge: 60 minutes

BASIC PRODUCT KNOWLEDGE MINI-MODULE

Materials

- ◆ Training Instrument 3–1: Product Knowledge Worksheet

- ◆ Tool 3–1: Worksheet Example A: Product Knowledge

- ◆ Tool 3–2: Worksheet Example B: Product Knowledge

Individual Work

Provide Training Instrument 3–1 for the salespeople to use. A typical assignment would be to have the salespeople complete their worksheets using the actual products/services that they will sell. Within a specified amount of time they should meet with their managers to review their worksheets for accuracy. The number of products/services targeted for sale determines the timeframe of the assignment.

Group Work

Group work can be done with a mix of new and experienced salespeople. A group of all new sales personnel will need to have some information available, such as product manuals, brochures, customer comments, and so forth. For a group of experienced salespeople, the exercise is intended to sharpen knowledge. The following is a suggested exercise.

Structured Exercise 3–7

Step 1: Preselect the products/services to be used in the exercise.

Step 2: Split the class into groups of three to five people and hand out the training instrument.

Step 3: Split up the products/services among the groups and ask each group to fill out the worksheet (base the time on how many products/services each group has).

Step 4: When each group has completed its worksheet, ask each group to select a spokesperson to share its work with the class.

Step 5: Collect the sheets at the end of the exercise and type them up for distribution to the participants.

To create alignment among the participants about determining the purpose of a feature that is used on the worksheets, you can use the following distinction: the purpose of a feature is what makes the feature a benefit or an advantage that the customer believes is a benefit or an advantage.

BASIC COMPETITOR KNOWLEDGE MINI-MODULE

Materials

- ◆ Training Instrument 3–2: Competitor Knowledge Worksheet

- ◆ Training Instrument 3–3: Top Competitors Summary Worksheet

- ◆ Tool 3–3: Worksheet Example: Competitor Knowledge

- ◆ Tool 3–4: Worksheet Example: Top Competitors Summary

Using the Materials in This Mini-Module

Training Instrument 3–2: Competitor Knowledge Worksheet requires salespeople to obtain information about a competitor during a period of one to two months. You can launch this project as pre-session work or you may choose to launch it during a training session and follow up later. Tool 3–3 is a sample worksheet filled out for your reference.

You can use Training Instrument 3–3: Top Competitors Summary Worksheet within a training situation with access to public information about the competitor (data via Internet, annual reports, articles, sales files, and so forth).

On Training Instrument 3–3, the terms *Strengths, Weaknesses, Opportunities,* and *Threats* are about the competitor. To complete the worksheet, salespeople should brainstorm about the competitor's overall strengths, weaknesses, opportunities, and threats. A common mistake is to fill in the competitor's strengths, weaknesses, opportunities, and threats only in relation to your organization. This exercise enables participants to see the competitors in a more holistic light.

Tools 3–3 and 3–4 are completed worksheet examples you may use for reference.

Structured Exercise 3–8

Step 1: Preselect the competitors (or ask the group to select them) for the exercise.

Step 2: Split the class into groups of three to five people and hand out Training Instrument 3–3 to each group. Provide any information on the competitors. (Internet access is ideal.)

Step 3: Split the competitors among the groups and ask each group to fill out its worksheet. Allow appropriate time based on the number of competitors each group works with.

Step 4: Ask each group to select a spokesperson to share its work with the class.

Step 5: Collect the sheets at the end of the exercise and type them up for distribution to the participants.

BASIC CUSTOMER KNOWLEDGE MINI-MODULE

Materials

- Training Instrument 3–4: Individual and Corporate Customer Knowledge Worksheet

- Tool 3–5: Worksheet Example: Individual and Corporate Customer Knowledge

Using the Materials in This Mini-Module

Completion of Training Instrument 3–4 may require several visits with a customer, and thus using this worksheet in training is limited to two possibilities:

1. talking about the ways that the participants can use information about a customer.

2. finding out as much information as possible before seeing the customer.

These activities are outlined in the following two structured exercises.

Structured Exercise 3–9

Why Customer Information Is Important (5–10 minutes)

Step 1: Separate the class into pairs or groups of three to five people and hand out Tool 3–5 to each group. Split up the worksheet among the groups so that each group works on different sections.

Step 2: For each topic, ask groups to determine one or two reasons why this information is important.

Step 3: When the worksheets are completed, ask each group to select a spokesperson to share its work with the class.

Step 4: Collect the sheets at the end of the exercise and type them up for distribution to the participants.

Structured Exercise 3–10

Individual Work

Step 1: Hand out Training Instrument 3–4 to each salesperson.

Step 2: Using available information, have the salesperson complete the worksheet.

Step 3: Instruct each salesperson to review the worksheet for accuracy with her or his manager within a specified period of time. The timeframe to complete this assignment depends on the number of customers assigned.

Group Work (20–60 minutes, depending on the number of customers assigned and the detail expected)

Step 1: Preselect the customers to be used in the exercise or ask the group to select them.

Step 2: Split the class into pairs or groups of three to five people and distribute Training Instrument 3–4 to each group.

Step 3: Divide the customers among the groups. Provide any information about customers. (Internet access is ideal.)

Step 4: Ask each group to fill out its worksheet. Base the amount of time provided on how many customers each group has.

Step 5: When the worksheets are complete, ask each group to select a spokesperson to share its work with the class.

Step 6: Collect the sheets at the end of the exercise and type them up for distribution to the participants.

What to Do Next

- Look at Table 1–1: Sales Training Modules Matrix to determine how best to use the modules in this chapter and to identify the type of sales personnel who would benefit. You can review this matrix and the sales gap analysis completed by the sales personnel to decide which other modules you might want to use with the modules from this chapter. Also review the material in chapter 1 on how best to use this book according to your situation.

- For the first few modules you facilitate, plan on one hour of preparation for every hour of facilitation. As you gain experience with the modules, plan on 20 minutes for every hour of facilitation.

- Determine the time available for the training session. Schedule the session. Arrange for the facility and audiovisual equipment (projector, screen, sound system), flipcharts with paper, colored markers, and so forth.

- Determine food and beverage requirements and make necessary arrangements.

- Invite participants. Send confirmation with an agenda or a list of the modules to be covered.

- Prepare training materials to match your enrollment.

- Practice. Carefully review the training materials. Be prepared to respond to questions that the materials and activities are likely to generate. Review the PowerPoint presentation and practice in front of a friend or colleague to make yourself comfortable with the key points and slide transitions and to solidify your understanding of the topic.

- On the basis of the number of participants, determine how you will conduct the structured exercises (in pairs, trios, or small groups) and the method you will use for splitting the class into working groups (for example, counting off, find your own partner, and so forth).

- For discussion questions, prepare answers to help the group share their ideas (to prime the pump) and use real-life scenarios from your organization.

- ◆ As much as possible, check all arrangements in the training room either the night before training starts or two to three hours prior to the start of the session.

- ◆ Prepare the evaluation form (see Appendix B) for the attendees so that you can receive feedback and have information for improving the module for future training sessions.

- ◆ After the session, provide the evaluation results and any post-training assignments to the participants' managers. You also may wish to provide a summary report of any insights you obtained during the training.

◆ ◆ ◆

Now that you have an understanding of the basics of the sales process, it's time to move on to the aspects that will improve productivity. The next chapter includes a module that teaches you how to challenge the way salespeople think and encourage them to differentiate between assumptions and facts—an essential element to understanding what makes your customers tick.

Training Instrument 3–1
Product Knowledge Worksheet

PRODUCT/SERVICE	FEATURE	WHAT THE FEATURE DOES	PURPOSE OF THE FEATURE	PRICE

Training Instrument 3–2
Competitor Knowledge Worksheet

Name of Competitor: _____ Date: _____

Headquarters location	
Web address	
Public, private, or subsidiary? (If subsidiary, of whom?)	
Fiscal or calendar year? (If fiscal year, what is the time period?)	
Last year's revenues and profits	
Stock performance over past 12 to 24 months	
Dun & Bradstreet rating	
Financial condition	
Organizational structure	
Key people	
Number of employees	
Number of locations	
Key products	
Prices of key products	
Pricing history	
Target markets	
Distribution mechanisms	

continued on next page

Training Instrument 3–2, continued

Competitor Knowledge Worksheet

Market share	
Marketing activities	
Short-term strategy	
Long-term strategy	
Topic of any recent articles or news releases (put copies in the file)	
Key accounts (name, salesperson, revenue) and those we want	
Customer comments (quality, service delivery, problem resolution)	
Perception of our firm	
Ways to beat this competitor (maximum of five)	

Training Instrument 3–3
Top Competitors Summary Worksheet

Competitor			
Product			
Price			
Distribution			
Strengths			
Weaknesses			
Opportunities			
Threats			
Other			

Training Instrument 3–4

Individual and Corporate Customer Knowledge Worksheet

Name of Customer: _____ Date: _____

Birth date	
Hometown	
Education	
Family information	
Special interests	
Sensitive issues	
Career information	
Current boss and peer information	
Other people in our firm who know this person, and how?	
Primary job responsibility	
Job performance is based on . . . (business objectives)	
Authority levels	

continued on next page

Training Instrument 3–4, continued
Individual and Corporate Customer Knowledge Worksheet

Opinions (of you, our firm, our competitors)	
People orientation	
Thinking style	
Key problems, concerns, and challenges	
Priorities (customer and management)	
Our solutions	
Competitors' solutions	
Other information	
Public, private, or subsidiary (If subsidiary, of whom?)	
Years in business and nature of business	
Fiscal or calendar year? (If fiscal year, what is the time period?)	

continued on next page

Training Instrument 3–4, continued
Individual and Corporate Customer Knowledge Worksheet

Last year's revenues and profits	
Stock performance over past 12 to 24 months	
Dun & Bradstreet rating	
Financial condition	
Organizational structure	
Key people	
Number of employees	
Number of locations	
Key products	
Target markets	
Distribution mechanism	
Market share	
Marketing activities	

continued on next page

Training Instrument 3–4, continued
Individual and Corporate Customer Knowledge Worksheet

Short-term strategy	
Long-term strategy	
Key business issues	
Topic of any recent articles or news releases (put copies in the file)	
Key customers	

Tool 3–1
Worksheet Example A: Product Knowledge

PRODUCT/SERVICE	FEATURE	WHAT THE FEATURE DOES	PURPOSE OF THE FEATURE	PRICE
What your organization sells to your customers:	Prominent part or characteristic of the product/service:	The intention or outcome of the feature or a technical aspect:	What makes it better for the customer (the potential benefit):	
◆ software	◆ calculates ROI	◆ automatic calculation	◆ faster approval process	◆ Included
◆ accounting services	◆ tax calculation included	◆ provides tax services at no extra fee	◆ no hidden fees	◆ Included
◆ hamburgers	◆ cooked to order	◆ customized cooking	◆ satisfy each customer's taste	◆ $x.xx
◆ hotel rooms	◆ soundproof walls	◆ peaceful sleeping	◆ be rested for the day's activities	◆ $xxx.xx
◆ overnight delivery	◆ delivered before 10 a.m.	◆ timely delivery	◆ no wasted time waiting for letter	◆ $xx.xx
◆ women's sports clothing	◆ carries all sizes, guaranteed	◆ handle all customer sizes	◆ one-stop shopping	◆ N/A
◆ auto insurance	◆ 24-hour settlement	◆ get cars on the road fast	◆ one less hassle in life	◆ Extra
◆ real estate	◆ largest selection in town	◆ provide a wide selection	◆ find your new home faster	◆ N/A
◆ financing	◆ approved on the spot	◆ customer can purchase now	◆ know now if you can buy	◆ N/A
◆ consulting services	◆ guaranteed results	◆ reduces risk	◆ solutions that work	◆ Included

N/A = Not applicable.

Tool 3–2

Worksheet Example B: Product Knowledge

PRODUCT/SERVICE	FEATURE	WHAT THE FEATURE DOES	PURPOSE OF THE FEATURE	PRICE
Spam software	Challenge response	Learns your friends and enemies and adapts to your email characteristics, without complicated rules or settings	Gives the user control over email	$xx.xx
Half-fold envelope	8.5 × 11-inch paper folds once	Allows 8.5 × 11-inch paper or card stock to be used as a greeting card or one-fold brochure	Lets users create their own cards and brochures	$x.xx for x
Customer service	24-hour customer service via a toll-free number	Operators answer all questions regarding the use of our services	Provides fast and effective service for our customers	Included in purchase price
Ergonomic hammer	Slip-resistant handle	Using space technology, the grip resists slippage and does not add extra weight to the hammer	Eliminates the possibility of the hammer slipping out your hand and causing an injury	$xx.xx
Lawn mower	Rear bag	Catches cut grass behind the mower	Enables the mower to cut along the side of fences or objects from either side	Included in purchase price

Tool 3–3

Worksheet Example: Competitor Knowledge

Name of Competitor: *Cheapo Tools*   Date: *July 2004*

Headquarters location	Somewhere, USA
Web address	www.cheapotools.com
Public, private, or subsidiary? (If subsidiary, of whom?)	Public
Fiscal or calendar year? (If fiscal year, what is the time period?)	Calendar year
Last year's revenues and profits	Revenue $100 million; profit $15 million
Stock performance over past 12 to 24 months	High: 12.5 one year ago Low: 3.5 last month Latest: 6.4
Dun & Bradstreet rating	3R3
Financial condition	Annual report shows that debt service takes 25 percent of revenues. This is above average for a firm this size according to Dun & Bradstreet
Organizational structure	Chairman*, president/CEO*, vice president of finance*, vice president of operations, vice president of sales and marketing; U.S. broken into three regions with regional managers for each *Sits on board of directors.
Key people	President and vice president of finance
Number of employees	125
Number of locations	one
Key products	Ergonomic tool line
Prices of key products	$xx.xx for hammer, $xx.xx for wrench

continued on next page

Tool 3–3, continued
Worksheet Example: Competitor Knowledge

Pricing history	No price increases in the past 15 months
Target markets	Neighborhood hardware stores in urban areas and markets where the big stores have not reached
Distribution mechanisms	Direct sales to hardware stores, no e-commerce
Market share	Unable to obtain
Marketing activities	Provides posters for stores, quarterly newsletter called the *Small Hardware Retailer,* no advertising
Short-term strategy	Expand into mountain states and Northwest agricultural areas
Long-term strategy	Continue to be the low-price provider
Topic of any recent articles or news releases (put copies in the file)	No articles; recent news releases were about new appointments (president/CEO and vice president of finance) following the purchase of the firm
Key accounts (name, salesperson, revenue) and those we want	XYZ Hardware stores, John Doe, unable to obtain revenue (however, they cover 85 percent of hardware stores in the Northeast). This is a target account for us. ABC Hardware stores, Jane Doe, annual report shows $1 million. Stores in the Southeast are not a target area for us.
Customer comments (quality, service delivery, problem resolution)	Complaints about quality of tools when used frequently. Customers wanted rebates, not another tool (source: JKL Independent Testing Service). No complaints for service delivery from stores.
Perception of our firm	Had lunch with John Doe and he said that we were not viewed as primary competitor because of our pricing.
Ways to beat this competitor (maximum of five)	(1) Quality; (2) better replacement policy; (3) joint promotions with hardware store owners during spring/summer

Tool 3–4

Worksheet Example: Top Competitors Summary

Competitor	Spam Killer	Cheapo Tools	Biz Office Furniture, Inc.
Product	Spam software	Ergonomic hammer	Office chair
Price	$xx.xx	$xx.xx	$xxx.xx
Distribution	Website only	Neighborhood hardware stores	Up-market stores, Website, Amazon, eBay
Strengths	Fast download from Website; purchased lead position on major search engines	Lowest price	Brand awareness; design awards; Website sales are increasing
Weaknesses	No challenge feature; software does not train itself	Hammer not designed for contractor use; rather, it's for infrequent use by homeowners	Pricing precludes them from more mass distribution through office supply stores such as Staples
Opportunities	As the low-cost provider, Spam Killer can grab market share fast	Become a provider to Wal-Mart	Increase in home-based businesses has increased demand for well-designed and functional chairs
Threats	Lack of features will make it difficult to break into corporate market	Their traditional base of neighborhood stores is becoming concerned about quality and safety	Continued decline in office building rentals reduces the demand for large purchases like those experienced in the 1990s
Other	Product ranked as "average" by *Hi-Tech* magazine	Company has been sold three times during the past 10 years	Stock has been stagnant through recent bull market; good public relations effort with new product

Tool 3–5

Worksheet Example: Individual and Corporate Customer Knowledge

Name of Customer: *Chris Jones, Spam Stopper*   Date: *July 2004*

Birth date	August 22, 1966
Hometown	Somewhere, USA
Education	BS (software engineering) from Appalachia State; MBA from University of North Carolina
Family information	Married (John) and two children (Sally, 5, and James, 2)
Special interests	Soccer, children's activities, and local symphony
Sensitive issues	None that I am aware of. Our conversations are primarily business related, and she does not bring up anything of a personal nature.
Career information	Worked for various software firms as a software engineer. At her last position (chief software engineer at XYZ Corp.), she started to become interested in managing a company and obtained her MBA. Current position is manager of new products.
Current boss and peer information	Reports directly to COO, has two peers (operations manager and director of marketing), and has a division of 25 employees (mostly engineers).
Other people in our firm who know this person, and why	Vice president of marketing; Chris's daughter Sally goes to school with VP's son.
Primary job responsibility	Development of new products with emphasis on innovation
Job performance is based on . . . (business objectives)	Number of new products delivered and revenue from these products
Authority levels	Can spend up to $250,000 without approval of chief operating officer.

continued on next page

Tool 3–5, continued

Worksheet Example: Individual and Corporate Customer Knowledge

Opinions (of you, our firm, our competitors)	When I have asked her if I am providing the service she requires, I get a polite yes, and then she continues the conversation. On three occasions she has stated that she appreciates our customer service, but she always qualifies this with a request for improved quality. She talks about the competition only when the annual contract comes up for review.
People orientation	Introverted. She likes to hear other opinions to test her own thinking. She is not too worried about what other people think of her.
Thinking style	Analytical (always looking at the numbers), and she always wants to get to the point.
Key problems, concerns, and challenges	Turnover of her staff. Competition has turned out two more successful products in the past two years.
Priorities (customer and management)	Chris's priority is to reduce turnover and management's is to get three or four new products ready for next calendar year.
Our solutions	Innovation process that engages staff so that they produce more products faster, which motivates them to stay.
Competitors' solutions	Similar, but without the track record we have
Other information	
Public, private, or subsidiary? (If subsidiary, of whom?)	Private
Years in business and nature of business	Five years. Software development to stop spam. They are now looking to get into other fields of software to help improve productivity.
Fiscal or calendar year? (If fiscal year, what is the time period?)	Calendar year

continued on next page

Tool 3–5, continued

Worksheet Example: Individual and Corporate Customer Knowledge

Last year's revenues and profits	No accurate reports because they are privately held; however, Chris said they had broken the $150 million mark last year.
Stock performance over past 12 to 24 months	Not available
Dun & Bradstreet rating	1R3
Financial condition	According to Dun & Bradstreet they are not a credit risk based on their payment history. Unable to get any other information.
Organizational structure	Chairman, president and chief executive officer is the main investor, COO, and then managers of divisions (COO and managers make up executive committee).
Key people	CEO, COO, and finance manager
Number of employees	55
Number of locations	One
Key products	Spam Killer and email sifter software
Target markets	End users; moving into corporate sales
Distribution mechanism	Website for end users; direct sales to corporate markets
Market share	Chris says they have a 35 percent share this year versus 38 percent last year.
Marketing activities	Advertise in trade publications
Short-term strategy	Increase market share of Spam Stopper to 40 percent through price reductions
Long-term strategy	Move out of spam software business and get into office productivity software
Key business issues	Spam segment getting crowded; key competitor Spam Killer was bought by a large conglomerate and has increased its marketing activities by 50 percent.

continued on next page

Tool 3–5, continued

Worksheet Example: Individual and Corporate Customer Knowledge

Topic of any recent articles or news releases (put copies in the files)	Crowded spam segment; the fight between Spam Stopper and Spam Killer; news releases on appointments and new email sifter program
Key customers	Currently have 10 corporate clients, with XYZ purchasing more software than the other nine combined. ABC Corp. is the largest user of email sifter.

Slide 3–1

Selling Today

"There are worse things in life than death. Have you ever spent an evening with an insurance salesman?"

– Woody Allen

Slide 3–2

Selling Today

World of Oversupply
- More choices
- More information about those choices

Result
- Customers want to deal with salespeople who will help them and not just "sell to them."
- Customers want the salesperson to add value.

Slide 3–3

Adding Value

- In groups, talk about ideas that would add value for your customers in the sales process.

- After 10–15 minutes, select a spokesperson for your group and present ideas to the class.

Slide 3–4

Customer Focus and You

While adding value for our customers, what else do we need to keep track of as part of being a professional salesperson?

Slide 3–5

Customer Focus and You

End of the Module

Slide 3–6

Effective Selling

"Do, or do not. There is no try."

– Yoda, The Empire Strikes Back

Slide 3–7

Effective Selling

A salesperson has the knowledge or ability to
- match the right product/service/solution to the right customer at the right price
- communicate effectively
- think and act strategically
- proactively build the effective customer relationships.

Slide 3–8

Effective Selling

What are the attributes and activities associated with matching the right product/service solution to the right customer at the right price?

Slide 3–9

Effective Selling

What are the attributes and activities associated with communicating effectively?

Slide 3–10

Effective Selling

What are the attributes and activities associated with thinking and acting strategically?

Slide 3–11

Effective Selling

What are the attributes and activities associated with building effective relationships with customers?

Slide 3–12

Effective Selling

End of the Module

Slide 3–13

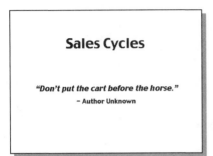

Sales Cycles

"Don't put the cart before the horse."
– Author Unknown

Slide 3–14

Slide 3–15

Slide 3–16

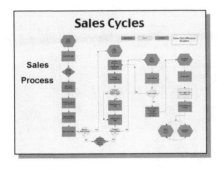

Slide 3–17

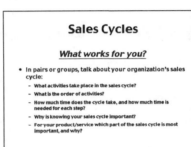

Slide 3–18

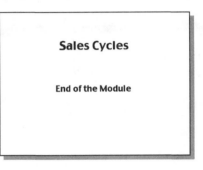

Thinking:
Sales Mind Focus Module

What's in This Chapter?

- ◆ A sales module that helps salespeople challenge the way they think and improve productivity

- ◆ A detailed explanation of how to eliminate autopilot decisions and focus on each customer

- ◆ A concise method for differentiating between assumptions and facts

This module may be the most important one in this book. It offers a disciplined thinking method that anyone can use to bring his or her background thinking into the foreground for examination and improvement. This module, which is based on work done by John L. Austin of Oxford University, Chris Argyris of Harvard University, Peter Senge of the Massachusetts Institute of Technology, and modern-day philosopher Fernando Flores, will help salespeople become more effective in all aspects of their job.

The module challenges salespeople to test their thinking. Although each day they think about products, service, and customers, too many decisions proceed automatically. Many of these autopilot decisions turn out okay and salespeople are lulled to sleep, blissfully unaware of how much better their thinking and decision making could become.

When a salesperson learns to improve his or her thinking, the results provide a sustainable advantage in every kind of situation and market.

Training Objective

This module provides a disciplined method of thinking that will improve a salesperson's productivity.

Key Points in This Module

◆ A sales mind focus lets the salesperson identify what she or he knows, doesn't know, and needs to know about a customer.

◆ Separating facts from opinions and assumptions helps direct effective action.

◆ Testing your thinking takes discipline and eliminates the autopilot mentality that limits potential.

Materials

◆ Two flipchart easels with paper and colored markers

◆ LCD projector, screen, and computer for running the PowerPoint presentation

◆ One tablet of paper and a pen or pencil for each participant

◆ PowerPoint slides 4–1 through 4–13. Copies of the slides for this module, *Sales Mind Focus.ppt,* are included at the end of this chapter.

◆ Each participant needs to bring information on two or three accounts or customers. (Participants who have taken the Basic Customer Knowledge mini-module in chapter 3 can use their completed worksheets.)

CD Resources

Materials for this module appear in this workbook and as electronic files on the accompanying CD. Insert the CD and open the "PDF Files" folder to locate electronic copies of the training instruments and tools mentioned in this chapter. The PowerPoint presentations are also on the CD. You will find more detailed instructions and help in locating files on the CD by referring to Appendix C, "Using the Compact Disc," at the back of the workbook.

Sample Agenda

9:00 a.m. Show slide 4–1. Yogi Berra, the former catcher and manager of the New York Yankees, is well known for his humorous and often meaningful quotes. An interpretation of the quote "We made too many wrong mistakes" is that the mistakes were avoidable. In the domain of

Table 4–1

Slide Information for the Sales Mind Focus Module

NUMBER	TITLE/TOPIC	DESCRIPTION	TIME
4–1	Title slide: Sales mind focus	Lets the class get settled and lets the facilitator welcome the group as appropriate	2–5 minutes
4–2	Why test your thinking?	Improved thinking	2–3 minutes
4–3	Facts and opinions	Definitions and examples	3–5 minutes
4–4	Sentence structure	Listening for facts and opinions; discussion questions	3–5 minutes
4–5	Directing effective action	The three "knows"; discussion question	1 minute
4–6	Practice	Structured exercise	2–3 minutes
4–7	Practice	Structured exercise	2–3 minutes
4–8	Practice	Structured exercise	3–5 minutes
4–9	Practice	Structured exercise	3–5 minutes
4–10	Practice	Structured exercise	3–5 minutes
4–11	Practice	Structured exercise	15–20 minutes
4–12	Recap	Structured exercise	10–15 minutes
4–13	End of the module		

sports, an avoidable mistake usually is related to what coaches call a mental error. The same can be said about selling. The mental errors related to taking action without identifying what we don't know are what create trouble or lost sales. This module identifies those avoidable mistakes through a disciplined-thinking methodology.

9:05   Show slide 4–2. Read the following information to the participants. If this is for individual training, let the salesperson read it from this workbook.

> *Every day at work you are engaged in thinking and making decisions that guide your actions. Too many decisions proceed automatically. Because many of these autopilot decisions turn out okay you are unaware of how much better your thinking and your decision making can become.*

Learning to improve your thinking gives you a sustainable advantage in every kind of situation and market.

To test and improve your thinking, first take automatic processes running in the background and bring them into the foreground where you can examine and analyze them. Under examination, you throw out old habits and thinking patterns that no longer serve you and thus sharpen your thinking.

Then you align this upgraded thinking to guide more disciplined actions. For example, to improve your driving, you first become aware of your driving habits (such as driving with one hand, not checking the side view mirrors, or turning on the directional signal after you've already started to change lanes). Only after you examine your driving habits can you consciously seek to improve. Often it takes a near accident or a police officer to alert us to the need for improvement. The same can be true of your thinking.

Typically, you become aware of the thinking that went into a decision only when you are questioned about the decision or when you get results you didn't expect.

9:10   Show slide 4–3. Read the following text to the participants. If this is for individual training, let the salesperson read the information from this workbook.

> *To improve the discipline in your thinking, you must first examine how you think, including the language in which you think. There are two key terms that deserve consideration:*

1. **Fact:** *objective, independent of the speaker, either true or false*

2. **Opinion/Assessment/Assumption:** *subjective, dependent on the speaker, based on a concern or on standards.*

Note to facilitator: You can provide some simple examples, such as:

◆ *I am 5 feet 8 inches tall.* Is this a fact? Yes. Why? Because we can measure my height and determine if the statement was true or false.

◆ *I am really tall.* Is this a fact? No. Why? Because it is based on my standards.

9:15   Show slide 4–4. Tell the participants that to help them further distinguish between facts and opinions, they have to be careful not to allow automatic listening to confuse them. Making this distinction is difficult because the sentence structure for a factual statement and that for an opinion are similar. Here are a few simple examples:

◆ This is a round table.

◆ This is a good table.

◆ The price is too high.

◆ The product does not answer our design criteria.

◆ I project *x* production from this account.

Following the questions on the slide, ask the participants

1. Which sentences are factual? Why?

Correct answers are

◆ This is a round table. The table either is round or it isn't.

◆ The product does not answer our design criteria. The design criteria provide a measurable standard.

2. Which sentences are opinions? Why?

Correct answers are

- This is a good table. "Good" has different definitions for different people and has different meanings in different situations. A good table for the task of writing may not be a good table around which to present your products.

- The price is too high. The speaker has a concern or standard for making this assessment, and the price might be okay for another customer. (**Note to facilitator:** This could be a factual statement for the customer if he or she could not qualify to purchase the product on the basis of set criteria, such as their budget or specifications.)

- I project *x* production from this account. Because the statement is about the future, it may be based on the standards of the speaker. In any event, one cannot say the projection is true or false because it has not yet happened.

3. Why is it important to make this distinction?

Answers you are looking for can include

- Understanding can change listening habits. When a customer says the price is too high, and we listen to it as an assessment, then we can ask why she or he thinks it's high instead of trying to prove that the price is right.

- Salespeople can reduce misunderstandings if they know that an opinion has been spoken.

9:20

Show slide 4–5. Say that the primary reason for testing our thinking is to give us the best chance to direct effective action based on these three simple questions:

1. What do I know about this customer?

2. What don't I know about this customer?

3. What do I need to know about this customer?

Ask the entire group the following question: How does answering those three questions direct effective action?

Possible answers are

◆ It identifies what sales personnel need to know and directs actions more effectively.

◆ It provides a deeper focus on each customer.

◆ It's not what we know that hurts us; it's what we don't know.

◆ Identifying what we don't know can help avoid missing the obvious.

◆ This can help us move through the sales cycle faster by not missing important information.

After you have received sufficient answers, go to the next slide.

9:25 Show slide 4–6. Tell the participants that they will start using the distinction between facts and opinions to specifically identify what they know about their customers.

Structured Exercise 4–1

Step 1: Split the class into pairs. (If you have an odd number, create one or two trios.)

Step 2: Have the pairs list all the facts they have on their accounts. Some examples are on the PowerPoint slide.

Step 3: After three to five minutes, ask the pairs to share what they factually know about their customers. As they share, pay attention to statements such as those that follow:

◆ "The customer said he likes us." Here is an important distinction: It is a fact that the customer said he likes us, but what was said is an opinion. Make sure the participants understand this distinction. Ask the pair who made this statement to share specifically what factual statements the customer made, and ask if there is any other factual evidence to support the customer's statement.

◆ "The customer will buy next week." This is an assumption. It can be converted to a fact by saying the customer has the contract and has stated that he will sign it next week.

◆ "The account is a good producer." This is an opinion based on some standard. If your firm has standards for rating accounts, use the ratings criteria to create a factual statement. For example, "This account produces x amount of revenue, which makes this an A account based on the rating criteria."

◆ "The customer likes the competition better." This is another assumption. A factual statement might be this one: "The customer says that she gives approximately 60 percent of her business to XYZ."

It is important to make sure the participants use facts for this exercise. If their initial work has mostly assumptions and opinions, ask them to redo the exercise and focus on facts. You can use the customer knowledge worksheet (Training Instrument 3–4) to help the participants.

9:35   Show slide 4–7. Say that in conjunction with slides 4–8 and 4–9, the class will now work on what they do not know.

Structured Exercise 4–2

Step 1: Using the same pairs of salespeople as in the previous exercise, ask participants to list all of their opinions, concerns, and assumptions about an account.

Step 2: After two or three minutes, ask each pair to share its work. Ideally you will hear some humorous statements, and everyone can laugh.

9:40   Show slide 4–8.

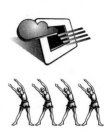

Structured Exercise 4–3

Step 1: Use the same pairs of salespeople. Have the pairs prioritize their opinions, concerns, and assumptions. (Those that are most important for getting the account's business should be at the top of the list.)

Step 2: Ask the participants to determine what facts, data, or past experiences they have to substantiate the most important three to five opinions, concerns, and assumptions. Remind them to be specific with their language and to avoid using opinions as substantiation.

Step 3: After three to five minutes, ask the pairs to share their work. Again, pay attention for opinions being used as substantiation. If an opinion is used, ask the salesperson if he or she can provide any factual evidence. If not, explain that an assumption is being made and save it for the next exercise.

9:50   Show slide 4–9. Tell the participants that the next two exercises will help them determine what they don't know.

Structured Exercise 4–4

Step 1: Continue to use the same pairs. Ask the pairs to determine which opinions, concerns, and assumptions have no evidence or factual substantiation.

Step 2: Ask them to talk together about what's missing. What information would help them bring this customer to the next stage?

Step 3: After three to five minutes, ask each pair to share its work with the group.

Step 4: Write the responses on a flipchart for future use with other modules or training follow-up.

10:00   Show slide 4–10. Practice, using the same pairs as in earlier exercises.

Structured Exercise 4–5

Step 1: Direct the participants to talk about what they need to know to move the customer to the next stage.

Step 2: For each item they should ask themselves why they need it. This will help prioritize the information they need. It is important for the participants to be critical in their thinking and specific with their statements.

Step 3: After three to five minutes, have each pair share its work with the group. Capture the work on flipcharts for future use in other modules or follow-up.

Step 4: When all the pairs have shared their work, ask for any comments or questions. At this point, it would be effective to have the pairs share their thinking about what the other pairs have shared. You will need to facilitate this group interaction so that one or two people do not dominate the conversation, which could happen if you have experienced salespeople mixed in with new salespeople.

10:10   Show slide 4–11. Say that the pairs now will develop an action plan for the accounts they have been working on in this module.

Structured Exercise 4–6

Step 1: Explain that each pair will develop an action plan for each account that it has been working on in this module. The action plans need to contain the following minimal information:

◆ name of the account

◆ facts about the account

◆ what the salesperson wants to accomplish with the account, and by when

◆ what stage the account is at (prospect, past user, and so forth)

◆ information the salesperson needs to take the account to the next stage

◆ actions to acquire this information, and by when.

Option: Ask the participants to type their action plans so they can distribute them to their colleagues as a reference tool.

Step 2: After 15–20 minutes, ask each pair to share its work with the group.

Step 3: After all the pairs have shared their work, ask for any comments or questions. Now is an effective time to have the pairs share their thinking about what the others have shared. You will need to facilitate this group interaction so that one or two people do not dominate the conversation, which could happen if you have experienced salespeople mixed in with novices.

10:30   Show slide 4–12. Tell the participants that the following exercise will help them capture their learning and prepare to use it on the job.

Structured Exercise 4–7

Step 1: Ask each pair to answer the questions on the slide.

Step 2: After 10–15 minutes, have each pair share its answers with the group.

Option: Ask the participants to type their answers so they can be given to their managers for follow-up.

10:45   Show slide 4–13. Explain that disciplined thinking will help avoid making "wrong mistakes." With today's fast pace of business, it will take practice to become disciplined thinkers. Tell participants if they practice every day, soon they will experience improvement.

What to Do Next

- ◆ Review Table 1–1: Sales Training Modules Matrix and the sales gap analyses completed by the sales personnel to determine which other modules you might want to use with the modules from this chapter. Also review the information in chapter 1 on how best to use this book to fit your situation.

- ◆ For the first few modules you facilitate, plan on one hour of preparation for every hour of facilitation. As you gain experience with the modules, plan on 20 minutes of preparation for every hour of facilitation.

- ◆ Determine how much time is available for the training session. Schedule the session. Arrange for the facility and audiovisual equipment (projector, screen, sound system, computer). Gather the other materials you will need.

- ◆ Determine food and beverage requirements and make necessary arrangements.

- ◆ Invite participants. Send confirmation with an agenda or a list of the modules to be covered.

- ◆ Practice. Carefully review the training materials. Be prepared to respond to questions that the materials and activities are likely to generate. Review the PowerPoint presentation and practice in front of a friend or colleague to become comfortable with the key points and slide transitions and to solidify your understanding of the topic.

◆ On the basis of the number of participants, determine how you will conduct the structured exercises (in pairs, trios, or small groups) and the method you will use for splitting the class into working groups (for example, counting off, letting each person find a partner, and the like).

◆ As much as possible, check all arrangements in the training room the night before (if training starts in the morning) or two to three hours prior to the start of the session.

◆ Prepare the evaluation form (see Appendix B) for the attendees so that you can receive feedback and have information for improving the module for future training sessions.

◆ After the session, provide the evaluation results and any post-training assignments to the participants' managers. You also may wish to provide a summary report of any insights you obtained during the training.

◆ ◆ ◆

Differentiating between assumptions and facts is the salesperson's first step toward understanding what makes customers tick. You can find the next steps in chapter 5, which addresses relationships between salespeople and customers.

Slide 4–1

Sales Mind Focus

"We made too many wrong mistakes."
– Yogi Berra

Slide 4–2

Sales Mind Focus

Why Test Your Thinking?

Slide 4–3

Sales Mind Focus

Facts – objective, independent of the speaker, either true or false

Opinions/Assessments/Assumptions – subjective, dependent on the speaker, based on standards and concerns

Slide 4–4

Sales Mind Focus

Sentence structures for a factual statement and an opinion are similar:

This is a round table.
This is a good table.
The price is too high.
The product does not answer our design criteria.
I project X production from this account.

Which sentences are factual? Why?
Which sentences are opinions? Why?
Why is it important to make this distinction?

Slide 4–5

Sales Mind Focus

Directing Effective Action

What do I know about this customer?

What don't I know about this customer?

What do I need to know about this customer?

How does answering the above questions direct effective action?

Slide 4–6

Sales Mind Focus
Practice

Using 1–2 accounts, customers, or prospects, list all the facts you have or know.

Some examples:
- Past business – contracted future business
- Customer satisfaction surveys
- Publicly available financial information
- Buying patterns

Slide 4–7

Sales Mind Focus
Practice

Now list all of your opinions, concerns, and assumptions.

Some examples:
- The customer will continue purchasing at the current level.
- Our new pricing structure will be a problem.
- The customer likes our product or I think she will like it.
- We will get this business.

Slide 4–8

Sales Mind Focus
Practice

Step 1. Prioritize your opinions, concerns, and assumptions.

Step 2. For the most important opinions, concerns, and assumptions, do your facts and past experience substantiate your opinions, concerns, and assumptions?

Be critical about your facts.
Avoid using opinions as substantiation.
Be specific with your language.

Slide 4–9

Sales Mind Focus
Practice

Now determine what you know and don't know by comparing your facts to your opinions and by asking yourself this simple question:

What's missing?

(What information would help me move this customer to the next stage?)

Slide 4–10

Sales Mind Focus
Practice

- Taking what you don't know about your customer, what do you need to know to move the customer to the next stage?

- For each item you need to know, ask yourself why you need to know it. This will help you prioritize. Again, be critical and specific.

Slide 4–11

Sales Mind Focus
Practice

- Using your prioritized list of what you need to know, develop an action plan with the following minimum information:
    - name of account
    - important facts about the account
    - what the salesperson wants to accomplish with the account, and by when
    - what stage the account is at (prospect, negotiating, user, and so on)
    - information the salesperson needs to take the account to the next stage
    - actions to acquire this information, and by when

Slide 4–12

Sales Mind Focus
Recap

- What have you learned from this module?
- What will you use right away in your work? Why?
- How will you use what you have learned?
- What is the effective way for you to test your thinking consistently and improve your actions? Why?
- Pick 2–3 accounts/customers with whom you will use this skill. By when will you use it?

Thinking: Managing Tasks and Relationships Module

What's in This Chapter?

- A sales module that address relationships between salespeople and customers

- A method to help salespeople balance relationship-building efforts and pending tasks

- An explanation of the two types of relationships: transactional and consultative

This module touches on an important aspect of selling today—relationships. With impatient customers armed with knowledge about a seller and his or her competitors, a salesperson not only has to take care of the task (providing information, sending proposals, and so forth); she or he also needs to understand the kind of relationship the customer expects. Both the task and the relationship have to be addressed; if not, the salesperson puts the business at risk.

Customers often describe salespeople in three categories:

1. The customer can really depend on the salesperson to perform, but there is no relationship between the two—*looks like too much focus on the task.*

2. The customer really likes the salesperson but can't count on him or her to get the job done—*looks like too much focus on the relationship.*

3. The customer says that the salesperson gets things done and makes her or him feel special—*ahhh . . . a balance between task and relationship.*

Whenever interaction between two people occurs, some type of relationship exists. How relationships form and how they are managed affect everyone involved. Interactions often focus on the tasks immediately at hand, and the relationship develops by default rather than by design. This lack of attention leaves the relationship open to breakdowns or makes it easy for a competitor to acquire the customer's business.

In this training module, we will focus on two major types of customer relationships: *transactional* and *consultative*. Recognizing the attributes of these relationships will help salespeople design productive interactions with their customers. It is through productive relationships that customer loyalty can be built.

Training Objective

The purpose of this module is to provide insights into the effective management of tasks and relationships.

Key Points in This Module

- Relationships happen—by design or default. Preparing for a relationship helps avoid the wasted time of repairing relationships.

- There are two basic types of business relationships between a customer and a salesperson: transactional and consultative. The customer always drives the type of relationship.

- A salesperson can determine the type of relationship a customer wants through his or her recognizable behavior.

- Different activities support each relationship type.

- A productive relationship with a customer means aligning the salesperson's activities with the type of relationship the customer wants.

Materials

- Two flipchart easels with paper and colored markers

- LCD projector, screen, and computer for running the PowerPoint presentation

- Paper for the participants to use in taking notes

◆ PowerPoint slides 5–1 through 5–17. Copies of the slides for this module, *Managing Tasks and Relationships.ppt,* are included at the end of this chapter.

CD Resources

The PowerPoint presentation for this module is on the CD that accompanies this workbook. Thumbnail versions of the slides are at the back of this chapter. You will find more detailed instructions and help in locating files on the CD by referring to Appendix C, "Using the Compact Disc," at the back of the workbook.

Sample Agenda

9:00 a.m.   Show slide 5–1. Harvey Mackay, a successful businessman and well-known business writer with an emphasis on selling, bases much of his success on relationships that his sales team developed with the firm's customers and on the consistent delivery on promises made. This module is about achieving the proper balance of task completion and relationship building and maintenance. Every customer wants his or her own balance of task and relationship, and the salesperson must discover this balance.

9:05   Show slide 5–2. Tell the participants that whenever we interact with others, some type of relationship occurs. How relationships are formed and managed affects outcomes. Interactions often focus on current tasks, and the relationship develops by default rather than by design. This leaves the relationship open to breakdowns and ripe for competitors.

When we prepare for a relationship, we can avoid the wasted time of repairing it later. This enables us to add more value for our customers and focus on more productive activities.

9:10   Show slide 5–3. Ask participants what their customers would say about them. After you have received a few answers (or if you don't get any answers), ask the following questions:

◆ Would customers say that you are reliable and get the job done?

◆ Would customers say they enjoy working with you because you are friendly and care for them?

◆ Would customers say that you take care of the details, know how to work effectively with them, and add value all the time?

There is no need to go into detail with the responses to the questions. The purpose is to get the participants thinking about how their customers might perceive them with regard to task and relationship.

9:15   Show slide 5–4. Let the group read the definitions on the slide and then ask if anyone has any questions or additions to the definitions. The purpose of definitions is to have alignment among the participants about what these words mean.

Option: You could ask the participants what is the "glue" in their relationships with customers.

9:20   Show slide 5–5. Tell participants that there are many types of relationships they can have with their customers. Say that in this course, you will focus on two types: transactional and consultative.

THE TRANSACTIONAL RELATIONSHIP

Ask the participants the following question: What are the attributes of a transactional relationship?

After a few responses, click to show the bullet points on the slide and review the five attributes that characterize a transactional relationship:

1. **Cost based:** Believing that he or she understands the product as well as, or better than, the salesperson, the customer focuses on price and little else.

Table 5–1

Slide Information for the Managing Tasks and Relationships Module

NUMBER	TITLE/TOPIC	DESCRIPTION	TIME
5–1	Title slide: Managing tasks and relationships	Enables the class to get settled and the facilitator to welcome the group as appropriate	2 minutes
5–2	Relationships happen	Design vs. default—prepare vs. repair	1 minute
5–3	What is your orientation?	Three discussion questions	5 minutes
5–4	Definitions	Task and relationship	1 minute
5–5	Types of relationships	Two discussion questions	2–3 minutes
5–6	Which relationship is better?	Depends …	1 minute
5–7	Transactional relationship	Structured exercise	5–10 minutes
5–8	Transactional relationship	Structured exercise	5–10 minutes
5–9	Consultative relationship	Structured exercise	5–10 minutes
5–10	Consultative relationship	Structured exercise	5–10 minutes
5–11	Transactional relationship	Structured exercise	5–10 minutes
5–12	Consultative relationship	Structured exercise	5–10 minutes
5–13	Practice	Structured exercise	10–15 minutes
5–14	Practice	Structured exercise	10–15 minutes
5–15	Practice	Structured exercise	10–15 minutes
5–16	Recap	Structured exercise	10–15 minutes
5–17	End of the module		

2. **Buyer–Seller:** The customer views the relationship as simply as possible—the salesperson is seen as someone with whom to conduct a transaction.

3. **Opposed:** The customer sometimes views the relationship as primarily adversarial—she or he wants to get the best price and knows the salesperson is trying to get the highest price. The customer does not see the salesperson as adding value.

4. **Task oriented:** The customer focuses on the tasks involved in making a purchase and on ways to minimize them.

5. **Minimal time investment:** The customer is in a hurry and if the salesperson takes too much of the customer's time, the sale may be at risk.

THE CONSULTATIVE RELATIONSHIP

Ask the participants this question: What are the attributes of a consultative relationship?

After a few responses, click to show the bullet points on the slide and review the five attributes that characterize a consultative relationship:

1. **Benefits oriented:** The customer wants to know the benefits of the product or service so he or she can make a price/value decision or understand the potential solutions available.

2. **Client–Adviser:** The customer views the salesperson as an adviser who can help in making a good decision—she or he wants the salesperson to help minimize risk.

3. **Cooperative:** The customer wants a collaborative relationship with the salesperson.

4. **Relationship oriented:** The customer seeks a relationship with the salesperson that adds value for both parties.

5. **Mutual time investment:** The customer expects the salesperson to match his or her time investment—if the customer has to spend more time on the relationship than the salesperson, the sale may be at risk.

9:25 Show slide 5–6. Which relationship is better?

It depends on the customer. The key point is that the customer determines the relationship, and it is best to work with the customer in the style with which she or he is comfortable.

Treating a consultative customer as if they wanted to be transactional puts the relationship at risk and vice versa.

9:30 Show slide 5–7.

Structured Exercise 5–1

Step 1: Split the participants into pairs or groups of three to five people.

Step 2: Ask the groups to discuss this question: What is the customer looking for in a transactional relationship? Give them five minutes to work.

Step 3: Ask a spokesperson from each group to share the group's answers.

Step 4: After all the groups have spoken, review the following five points to cover anything they have missed:

1. **Best price:** The customer wants the best price, as he or she defines it.

2. **Easy purchase:** The customer wants the salesperson to make it easy to buy.

3. **Availability:** The customer wants it now.

4. **Task focus:** The customer views the salesperson as someone to perform tasks for the buyer.

5. Minimal time investment: The customer doesn't want to invest time in a relationship with the seller.

9:40 Show slide 5–8.

Structured Exercise 5–2

Step 1: Split the participants into pairs or groups of three to five people.

Step 2: Have the groups discuss this question: How do you recognize a customer who wants a transactional relationship? Give them five minutes to work.

Step 3: Ask a spokesperson from each group to share the group's answers.

Step 4: After all the groups have spoken, review these six points to cover anything they have missed:

1. **Knows the product as well as or better than the salesperson does.** If the salesperson offers too much information about the product, the customer views it as a waste of time.

2. **Only wants the basics or a standard version of a product.** Up-selling without a logical reason can upset this type of customer.

3. **Views the product as easily substitutable.** The customer thinks that the product or service is no different from or better than the competitor's product.

4. **Has little time for salespeople.** This customer seems to dismiss salespeople.

5. **Is difficult to reach via phone or does not answer email messages.** This customer will answer calls or return messages

on his or her schedule and shows little respect for the salesperson's time.

6. **Wants to stay focused on tasks.** This customer does not like small talk. He or she wants to keep interactions focused on getting something accomplished. Exploratory sales calls with this customer take more time than the customer wants to invest.

9:50 Show slide 5–9.

Structured Exercise 5–3

Step 1: Split the participants into pairs or groups of three to five people.

Step 2: Have participants discuss this question: What is the customer looking for in a consultative relationship? Give them five minutes to work.

Step 3: Ask a spokesperson from each group to share the group's answers.

Step 4: After all the groups have spoken, review these six points on the slide in case they missed anything:

1. **Solutions.** The customer wants solutions and expects the salesperson to know the product and the customer's business well enough to offer solutions.

2. **Information to help with decision making.** The customer wants the salesperson to provide relevant information without being asked and wants the salesperson to act as an adviser.

3. **Options.** The customer wants options.

4. **Hidden capabilities.** The customer wants the salesperson to point out hidden capabilities of the product or service as it relates to the customer's situation.

5. **Customization.** The customer wants his or her experience customized.

6. **Equal time investment from the salesperson.** The customer wants the salesperson to match or exceed her or his time investment.

10:00   Show slide 5–10:

Structured Exercise 5–4

Step 1: Split the participants into pairs or groups of three to five people.

Step 2: Have participants answer this question: How do you recognize a customer who wants a consultative relationship? Give them five minutes to work.

Step 3: Ask a spokesperson from each group to share the group's answers.

Step 4: After all the groups have spoken, review the six points on the slide in case the class missed anything:

1. **Provides information about what he or she wants and why.** The customer gives information because she or he believes this will help the salesperson provide better service.

2. **Asks questions about the product or service being offered.** This customer is inquisitive.

3. **Is at ease answering questions.** The customer will answer questions salespeople ask and will appreciate questions that make him or her think.

4. **Has time to meet with a salesperson.** This customer likes to meet with salespeople who add value to his or her job.

5. **Is easy to reach via phone and answers email messages.** This customer respects the salesperson's time and effort.

6. **Shows an interest in developing a relationship.** The customer wants to know the salesperson on more than a business level and shows interest in family, hobbies, career, and so forth.

10:10   Show slide 5–11.

Structured Exercise 5–5

Step 1: Split the participants into pairs or groups of three to five people.

Step 2: Have the participants answer this question: What tasks best support a transactional relationship? Give them five minutes to work.

Step 3: Ask a spokesperson from each group to share the group's answers.

Step 4: After all groups have presented, review these six points in case any were missed:

1. **Getting well prepared.** To minimize time with the customer, learn as much as you can about the customer before making contact. This customer type often views salespeople as time wasters.

2. **Asking as few questions as possible.** The salesperson needs to limit his or her questions and focus on the customer or task. This type of customer can view open-ended and exploratory questions as a waste of time.

3. **Providing new information.** Because this customer thinks she or he knows as much as or more than the salesperson does, the customer does not want the salesperson repeating something that is already known.

4. **Responding to queries quickly.** The customer wants things fast.

5. **Making it easy to buy.** The salesperson fills out forms (credit applications), hand-delivers or picks up contracts to expedite the delivery, and provides services that the customer will deem quicker and better.

6. **Minimizing face-to-face meetings.** The more the salesperson can do by email and phone, the more he or she will be viewed as efficient. Save the face-to-face meetings for very important conversations.

10:20   Show slide 5–12.

Structured Exercise 5–6

Step 1: Split the participants into pairs or groups of three to five people.

Step 2: Have the participants answer this question: What activities best support a consultative relationship? Give them five minutes to work.

Step 3: Ask a spokesperson from each group to share the group's answers.

Step 4: You can use the six points on the slide after all the groups have spoken to cover any points the groups might have missed:

1. **Preparing in order to talk about solutions.** The salesperson conducts research on the customer's industry, challenges, and strategies so that she or he can offer solutions quickly. He or she then conducts research within the selling company to identify similar situations that can form a baseline for thinking.

2. **Using open-ended questions.** Open-ended questions that are well designed will be well

received by this type of customer. She or he literally wants you to help think through the challenges.

3. **Customizing presentations and offers.** The customer views customization as a reflection of the salesperson's professionalism and desire to build an effective relationship.

4. **Delivering progress updates.** The customer wants to be informed about the salesperson's progress with any agreed-upon action steps.

5. **Having more face-to-face meetings.** The customer likes a personal touch the best.

10:45 Show slide 5–13.

Structured Exercise 5–7

Step 1: Split the group into pairs.

Step 2: Have each pair identify two or three accounts with whom they have transactional relationships and two or three accounts with whom they have consultative relationships. Then have the pairs answer this question: What action can you take to be more effective with these accounts? After 5–10 minutes ask each pair to report its ideas. You may want to capture these ideas on a flipchart.

11:00 Show slide 5–14.

Structured Exercise 5–8

Step 1: Keep the same pairs as you had in the previous exercise.

Step 2: Have pairs discuss each of the questions on Power-Point slide 5–14. Allow 10 minutes.

   ◆   When would a transactional relationship be at risk, and how would you know?

◆ Identify two or three accounts that are at risk, and develop two or three action steps to repair each relationship.

◆ When would a consultative relationship be at risk, and how would you know?

◆ Identify two or three accounts that are at risk, and develop two or three action steps to repair each relationship.

Step 3: Have each pair report its ideas to the group. You may want to capture these ideas on a flipchart.

11:15 Show slide 5–15. Let the participants read the Power-Point slide and then ask if anyone has other thoughts to add.

11:30 Show slide 5–16.

Structured Exercise 5–9

Step 1: Ask each pair to answer the questions on the slide. Allow 5–10 minutes.

Step 2: Have each pair share its answers.

Option: Ask the participants to write out their answers so they can be given to their managers for follow-up after the training.

11:40 Show slide 5–17.

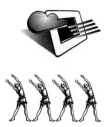

What to Do Next

◆ Table 1–1: Sales Training Modules Matrix will help you determine how best to use the module in this chapter and the type of sales personnel who would benefit from it. Review this matrix and the sales gap analyses completed by the sales personnel to identify which other modules to use with the material from this chapter.

◆ For the first few modules you facilitate, plan on one hour of preparation for every hour of facilitation. As you gain experience with the modules, plan on 20 minutes of preparation for every hour of facilitation.

◆ Determine the time available for the training session. Schedule the session. Arrange for the facility, audiovisual equipment (projector, screen, sound system) and other needed materials.

◆ Determine the food and beverage requirements and make necessary arrangements.

◆ Invite participants. Send confirmation with an agenda or the modules to be covered.

◆ Practice. Carefully review the PowerPoint slides and practice in front of a friend or colleague to become comfortable with the key points and slide transitions and to solidify your understanding of the topic. Be prepared to respond to questions that the activities are likely to generate.

◆ Based on the number of participants, determine how you will conduct the structured exercises (in pairs, trios, or small groups) and the method you will use for splitting the class into working groups (counting off, asking each participant to find a partner, and so forth).

◆ As much as possible, check all arrangements in the training room the night before if training starts in the morning, or two to three hours prior to the start of the session.

◆ Prepare the evaluation form (see Appendix B) for the attendees so that you can receive feedback and have information for improving the module for future training sessions.

◆ After the session, give the evaluation results and any post-training assignments to the participants' managers. You also may wish to provide a summary report of any insights you obtained during the training.

◆ ◆ ◆

Now that you understand the basics of relationship building, check out chapter 6 to learn ways to help salespeople discern what customers need in order to feel satisfied. When salespeople understand their customers' conditions of satisfaction, they'll be able to better meet customer needs and complete the sale.

Slide 5–1

Managing Tasks and Relationships

"People can't truly care how much you know until they know how much you care."
– Harvey Mackay

Slide 5–2

Managing Tasks and Relationships

Relationships Happen

Design vs. Default

Prepare vs. Repair

Slide 5–3

Managing Tasks and Relationships

What Is Your Orientation?

• Task
• Relationship
• Task and relationship

Slide 5–4

Managing Tasks and Relationships

Definitions

• Task – a piece of work often to be finished within a certain time

• Relationship – the relation connecting or binding participants in a relationship

Source: *Merriam-Webster's Collegiate Dictionary*, 11th ed.

Slide 5–5

Managing Tasks and Relationships

Types of Relationships

• Transactional
  – Cost based
  – Buyer–Seller
  – Opposed
  – Task oriented
  – Time investment is minimal

• Consultative
  – Benefits oriented
  – Client–Adviser
  – Cooperative
  – Relationship oriented
  – Time investment is matching

Slide 5–6

Managing Tasks and Relationships

Which relationship is better?

It depends on the customer...

Slide 5–7

Managing Tasks and Relationships

• What is the customer looking for in a transactional relationship?

  – Best price
  – Easy purchase
  – Availability
  – Task focus
  – Minimal time investment with salesperson

Slide 5–8

Managing Tasks and Relationships

• How do you recognize a customer who only wants a transactional relationship?

  – Knows the product as well as or better than the salesperson
  – Only wants the basics or a standard version of a product
  – Views the product as easily substitutable
  – Has little time for salespeople
  – Is difficult to reach via phone or does not answer email messages
  – Wants to stay focused on tasks

Slide 5–9

Managing Tasks and Relationships

• What is the customer looking for in a consultative relationship?

  – Solutions
  – Information to help in making a decision
  – Options
  – Hidden capabilities
  – Customization
  – Equal time investment from the salesperson

Slide 5–10

Managing Tasks and Relationships

• How do you recognize a customer who only wants a consultative relationship?

  – Provides information about what he wants and why
  – Asks questions about the product/service being offered
  – Is at ease answering questions
  – Has time to meet with a salesperson
  – Is easy to reach via phone and answers email messages
  – Shows an interest in developing a relationship

Slide 5–11

Managing Tasks and Relationships

• What tasks/activities best support a transactional relationship?

  – Prepare in order to minimize time with the customer
  – Ask as few questions as possible
  – Provide new information
  – Respond to queries quickly
  – Make it easy to buy
  – Minimize face-to-face meetings

Slide 5–12

Managing Tasks and Relationships

• What tasks/activities best support a consultative type of relationship?

  – Prepare in order to talk about solutions
  – Use open-ended questions
  – Customize presentations and offers
  – Provide progress updates
  – Hold more face-to-face meetings

Slide 5–13

Practice

- Transactional relationship – identify 2–3 accounts
- Consultative relationship – identify 2–3 accounts
- What actions can you take to be more effective with these accounts?

Slide 5–14

Practice

- When would a transactional relationship be at risk, and how would you know?
  - Identify 2–3 accounts that are at risk and develop 2–3 action steps to repair the relationship.
- When would a consultative relationship be at risk, and how would you know?
  - Identify 2–3 accounts that are at risk and develop 2–3 action steps to repair the relationship.

Slide 5–15

A Last Thought

Human beings are not perfectly responsive; a consultative customer on one day can act like a transactional customer on another day. Also, a customer can blend the attributes of transactional and consultative relationships.

Keep your "human radar" on and be flexible.

Slide 5–16

Recap

- What have you learned from this module?
- What will you use right away in your work? Why?
- How will you use what you have learned?
- What is an effective way for you to actively improve relationships with your customers? Why?
- Pick 2–3 accounts/customers that you will use your new understanding of relationships. By when will you use them?
- How will you know your actions are producing results?

Slide 5–17

Managing Tasks and Relationships

End of the Module

Thinking: Conditions of Satisfaction Module

- ◆ A sales module that helps salespeople understand their clients criteria for satisfaction

- ◆ A comprehensive description of explicit vs. implicit conditions of satisfaction

- ◆ Exercises that help participants discover details about their own clients

Conditions of satisfaction represent the criteria customers use to evaluate a salesperson's offer. If the offer meets their conditions of satisfaction, they will buy, and if the offer does not, they will not buy.

Conditions of satisfaction can be either spoken and explicit ("I need to have the product by this date or there is no deal") or unspoken and implicit (the customer thinks that your brand will help his or her business image). Implicit conditions of satisfaction often are of an emotional nature. Studies show that customers make their purchases based on emotional reasons (implicit) and then justify the decision with logical reasons (explicit). To further complicate selling, customers often expect the salesperson to know their conditions of satisfaction—even if they don't communicate them! Being an expert at uncovering conditions of satisfaction can separate you from other sales organizations.

Training Objective

The objective of this module is to ensure that sales personnel understand the concept of conditions of satisfaction and the difference between explicit and implicit conditions.

Key Points in This Module

- ◆ Conditions of satisfaction are the reasons (emotional and logical) that customers make purchases.

- ◆ Most customers purchase for emotional reasons and justify their purchase with logical reasons.

- ◆ Implicit conditions of satisfaction are the unspoken conditions and often are of an emotional nature.

- ◆ Explicit conditions of satisfaction are spoken or written and often are of a logical nature.

- ◆ There are common implicit and explicit conditions of satisfaction among customers purchasing a similar product or service.

- ◆ In the Inquiry module in chapter 8 and the Communication modules in chapter 9, your salespeople will learn tools to uncover the conditions of satisfaction.

Note to facilitator: You should run this module the first time with a group of experienced salespeople or with a mixed group. After that you will have enough information to let an individual take this module.

Materials

- ◆ Two flipchart easels with paper and colored markers

- ◆ Extra flipchart paper and markers for the structured exercises

- ◆ LCD projector, screen, and computer for running the PowerPoint presentation

- ◆ Paper for the participants to use in taking notes and during structured exercises

- ◆ PowerPoint slides 6–1 through 6–8. Copies of the slides for this module, *Conditions of Satisfaction.ppt,* are included at the end of this chapter.

CD Resources

The PowerPoint presentation for this module is on the CD that accompanies this workbook. Thumbnail versions of the slides are at the back of this chapter. You will find more detailed instructions and help in locating files on the CD by referring to Appendix C, "Using the Compact Disc," at the back of the workbook.

Sample Agenda

9:00 a.m. Display slide 6–1 as the participants enter the room. When asked for the time, Yogi Berra said, "Do you mean now?" Reading Yogi's quote often brings smiles or a subtle laugh. In the context of this module, it is an important distinction. Yogi was seeking an implicit or unspoken condition of satisfaction. In this module we learn about explicit and implicit conditions of satisfaction.

9:05 Show slide 6–2 and make the following points to the participants:

◆ The customers' expectations are part of their conditions of satisfaction. The customers will determine

Table 6–1

Slide Information for the Conditions of Satisfaction Module

NUMBER	TITLE/TOPIC	DESCRIPTION	TIME
6–1	Title slide: Conditions of satisfaction	Lets the class get settled and lets the facilitator welcome the group as appropriate	2 minutes
6–2	Conditions of satisfaction	Expectations, concerns; implicit and explicit conditions	1 minute
6–3	Definitions	Implicit and explicit conditions	1 minute
6–4	Explicit conditions of satisfaction	Structured exercise	10–15 minutes
6–5	Implicit conditions of satisfaction	Structured exercise	10–15 minutes
6–6	Practice	Structured exercise	10–15 minutes
6–7	Recap	Structured exercise	10–15 minutes
6–8	End of the module		

whether a product or service meets their conditions of satisfaction.

◆ When customers say they have concerns, it is likely they believe the product or service solution does not meet their conditions of satisfaction, which can be either implicit or explicit. Often it is the implicit, or unspoken, conditions that are the most important.

9:10 Show slide 6–3 and make sure the participants understand both definitions. Note that the definitions of *implicit* and *explicit* are precise. The quote from Yogi Berra on the first slide is an example of an implicit situation. The person asking, "What time is it?" most likely had body language that suggested he wanted the current time. An example of an explicit sales situation would be a request for proposals that outlines the minimum requirements for purchase.

Tell the participants that these definitions will help them with the exercises in this module. Ask if there are any questions.

9:15 Show slide 6–4 and conduct the structured exercise. Say that the purpose of this exercise is to identify the common explicit and implicit conditions of satisfaction that we work with.

Structured Exercise 6–1

Step 1: Split the class into pairs or groups of three to five people, depending on the size of the class.

Step 2: Give them 10 minutes to come up with as many explicit conditions of satisfaction as they can. Provide the class with some examples of explicit conditions of satisfaction, such as these:

◆ technical or performance specifications

◆ delivery schedule

◆ payment terms (could also be implicit if there are industry norms or standards)

- exchange policy (could also be implicit)

- size of product or number of items

- price.

Step 3: Have each group select a spokesperson to present its work.

Step 4: Write the findings on a flipchart.

Note to facilitator: For individual learners, have the salesperson make a list of explicit conditions of satisfaction. (This also could be assigned as homework.) When he or she is done, review ideas that previous individuals or groups had.

9:30   Show slide 6–5.

Structured Exercise 6–2

Step 1: Split the class into pairs or groups of three to five people.

Step 2: Give them 10 minutes to come up with as many implicit conditions of satisfaction as they can. Give the class some examples of implicit conditions of satisfaction, such as these:

- security (could also be explicit)

- ego or social status (wants to look good)

- quality of the product/service (could also be explicit)

- does not want to be taken advantage of

- price is a good deal

- respect for time or the decision process (could also be explicit)

- no hassles

- treated with respect during the sales process.

Step 3: Have each group select a spokesperson to present its work.

Step 4: Write their findings on a flipchart.

Note to facilitator: For individual learners, have the salesperson make a list of implicit conditions of satisfaction. (This also could be assigned as homework.) When he or she is done, review ideas that previous individuals or groups had.

9:45 Show slide 6–6. Conduct the following structured exercise.

Structured Exercise 6–3

Step 1: Split the class into pairs and ask each pair to pick two or three customers.

Step 2: Give them 10–15 minutes to do the following:

- ◆ identify each customer's explicit and implicit conditions of satisfaction (including concerns and doubts)

- ◆ generate ideas for effectively addressing the explicit conditions of satisfaction

- ◆ generate ideas for effectively addressing the implicit conditions of satisfaction.

Step 3: Have pairs share their work with the class.

Step 4: Write what the pairs share on a flipchart.

Note to facilitator: For individual learners, ask the salesperson to choose one or two customers. Have her or him identify each customer's explicit and implicit conditions of satisfaction and list ways to address them. (This also could be assigned as homework.) When the salesperson is done, review the lists from past classes.

10:00 Show slide 6–7. Say that the purpose of this exercise is to help the participants capture their learning and prepare to use their new knowledge on the job.

Structured Exercise 6–4

Step 1: In their previous pairs, ask participants to discuss the questions on the slide.

Step 2: After 10–15 minutes ask each pair to share its answers.

Option: Ask the participants to write out their answers so they can be given to their managers for follow-up after the training.

10:15   Display slide 6–8. In the Inquiry module in chapter 8 we will learn how to uncover implicit conditions of satisfaction, and in the Compelling Offers module in chapter 12 we will learn how to use these implicit conditions to our advantage in the sales process.

A final note: When we lose sales, it often is tied to a condition of satisfaction that was not met. Remember, it is what we do not know that hurts us.

What to Do Next

- ◆ Review Table 1–1: Sales Training Modules Matrix for help in determining how best to use the module in this chapter and the type of sales personnel who would benefit. Also review the matrix and the sales gap analyses completed by the sales personnel to determine which other modules you might want to use. Finally review the information in chapter 1 on how best to use this book to fit your situation.

- ◆ For the first few modules you facilitate, plan on one hour of preparation for every hour of facilitation. As you gain experience with the modules, plan on 20 minutes of preparation for every hour of facilitation.

- ◆ Determine how much time is available for the training session. Schedule the session. Arrange for the facility and audiovisual equipment (projector, sound system, computer). Gather the other materials you will need.

◆ Determine food and beverage requirements and make necessary arrangements.

◆ Invite participants. Send confirmation with an agenda or a list of the modules to be covered.

◆ Practice. Carefully review the training materials. Be prepared to respond to questions that the materials and activities are likely to generate. Review the PowerPoint presentation and practice in front of a friend or colleague so you're comfortable with the key points and slide transitions and have a solid understanding of the topic.

◆ Based on the number of participants, determine how you will conduct the structured exercises (in pairs, trios, or small groups) and the method you will use for splitting the class into working groups (for example, counting off, letting each person find a partner, and the like).

◆ As much as possible, check all arrangements in the training room the night before (if training starts in the morning), or two to three hours prior to the start of the session.

◆ Prepare the evaluation form (see Appendix B) for the attendees so that you can receive feedback and have information for improving the module for future training sessions.

◆ After the session, provide the evaluation results and any post-training assignments to the participants' managers. You also may wish to provide a summary report of any insights you obtained during the training.

◆◆◆

This chapter helped your salesforce become aware of implicit conditions of satisfaction, but that skill won't help a bit if salespeople can't manage their time appropriately. Use chapter 7 to train people to eliminate those pesky activities that do not contribute to productivity and to focus their time on things that will boost their sales numbers.

Slide 6–1

Conditions of Satisfaction

"Do you mean now?"
(when asked for the time)
– Yogi Berra

Slide 6–2

Conditions of Satisfaction

- Expectations
- Concerns and doubts

- Implicit
- Explicit

Slide 6–3

Conditions of Satisfaction

Definitions

- Implicit – *capable of being understood from something else, although not expressed or involved in the nature or essence of something; not revealed, expressed, or developed*

- Explicit – *fully revealed or expressed without vagueness, implication, or ambiguity; leaving no question as to meaning or intent*

Slide 6–4

Conditions of Satisfaction

What are the <u>explicit</u> conditions of satisfaction for your customers?

Slide 6–5

Conditions of Satisfaction

What are the <u>implicit</u> conditions of satisfaction for your customers?

Slide 6–6

Practice

- Pick 2–3 customers with whom you are working.
- Identify their explicit and implicit conditions of satisfaction.
- How can you effectively address the explicit conditions of satisfaction?
- How can you effectively address the implicit conditions of satisfaction?

Slide 6–7

Recap

- What have you learned from this module?
- What will you use right away in your work? Why?
- How will you use what you have learned?
- What is the effective way for you to seek out the customer's conditions of satisfaction consistently and to improve your actions? Why?
- Pick 2–3 accounts/customers on whom you will use this skill. By when will you use it?

Slide 6–8

Conditions of Satisfaction

End of the Module

Planning and Organizing Module

What's in This Chapter?

- A sales module that eliminates poor time-management habits

- An action plan to reduce activities that do not add value or increase productivity

- Individual exercises that highlight how a person spends his or her time

A frequent rhetorical question in a sales department is, "Where did my time go?" This module will help your salespeople answer that question and explore how to manage their schedules more productively.

We are all busy with meetings, paperwork, customer requests, sales calls, and much more. It's very easy to get caught up in our day-to-day work and forget to reflect on our actions to identify which activities help us achieve our goals. What a salesperson does with the time available to him or her often makes the difference in achieving goals. For most salespeople, even a small and consistent change in activities can have a significant impact on productivity.

Training Objective

This module provides an opportunity for salespeople to examine their activities and the way they allocate their time for those activities. Participants will develop an action plan to reduce those activities that do not add value to their productivity.

Key Points in This Module

- Examining our activities can reveal that some do not help us achieve our goals.

◆ Although some activities do not help salespeople meet their goals, they still need to be done (for example, filling out expense reports).

◆ For most salespeople, a wholesale change in activities is not needed—only incremental adjustments in the prioritization of activities.

Materials

◆ Two flipchart easels with paper and colored markers

◆ LCD projector, screen, and computer for running the PowerPoint presentation

◆ Paper for the participants to use in taking notes

◆ Training Instrument 7–1: Where Does My Time Go? Worksheet

◆ Tool 7–1: Worksheet Example: Where Does My Time Go?

◆ PowerPoint slides 7–1 through 7–7. Copies of the slides for this module, *Planning and Organizing.ppt,* are included at the end of this chapter.

CD Resources

Materials for this module appear both in this workbook and as electronic files on the CD that accompanies the book. To access the files, insert the CD and look at its "PDF Files" directory for the training instrument and tool needed. The PowerPoint presentation is also on the CD. Thumbnail versions of the slides appear at the back of this chapter. You will find more detailed instructions and help in locating files on the CD by referring to Appendix C, "Using the Compact Disc," at the back of the workbook.

Sample Agenda

9:00 a.m.   Show slide 7–1—another Yogi Berra quote, this time about planning. With our hectic day-to-day schedules we can get so busy that we lose sight of what we need to do to get where we want to go. Handling customer requests and complaints, completing paperwork, answering colleague requests, and all the other non-sales activities can seem so pressing that it is a wonder anyone has time for selling! This module uses a simple formula to help sales-

Table 7–1

Slide Information for the Planning and Organizing Module

NUMBER	TITLE/TOPIC	DESCRIPTION	TIME
7–1	Title slide: Planning and organizing	Enables the class to get settled and the facilitator to welcome the group as appropriate	2 minutes
7–2	Where does my time go?	Structured exercise	5–10 minutes
7–3	Where does my time go?	Structured exercise	2–3 minutes
7–4	Where does my time go?	Structured exercise	10–12 minutes
7–5	Where does my time go?	Structured exercise	3–5 minutes
7–6	Recap	Structured exercise	10–15 minutes
7–7	End of the module		

people keep focused on what they are hired to do—sell and produce revenue.

9:05   Show slides 7–2 through 7–5, which outline the following structured exercise.

Structured Exercise 7–1

Note to facilitator: Steps 1–5 are done on an individual basis rather than in pairs or small groups.

Step 1: Distribute Training Instrument 7–1: Where Does My Time Go? Worksheet

Note to facilitator: Use Tool 7–1 to lead the class.

Step 2: Ask the participants to list on Training Instrument 7–1 all the activities they are involved with during a typical week. See Tool 7–1 for examples.

Step 3: Tell the participants to place an "X" in one of the four columns to the right of each activity they listed on the worksheet (see Tool 7–1 for examples).

Step 4: Display slide 7–3. Tell the participants to write in the Adds Value box for each activity one of the three symbols displayed (see Tool 7–1 for examples):

- ◆ + adds value to my productivity

- ◆ = neutral to my productivity

- ◆ – subtracts value from my productivity.

After two or three minutes ask if anyone has any questions and help the participants complete the worksheet. Use Tool 7–1 as a guide to answering questions.

Step 5: Display slide 7–4 and ask the participants to review the "Not Important" activities they have marked on their worksheets. Ask, "Can any of these be changed?" After two or three minutes ask for volunteers to share some of the activities they could change or eliminate. **Note to facilitator:** If participants seem reluctant to speak up, ask them if there are activities they would like to change but do not think they have the authority to change. Explain that you will write these activities down and share them with management. When this is completed, ask, "What activities within your control can you change?" A pump-priming question could be, "What can you do when a colleague starts a social conversation and you are busy preparing for a call or writing a proposal?"

Step 6: Split the group into pairs.

Step 7: Have pairs share ideas that either eliminate the activity or reduce the time the activity takes. Allow 10 minutes.

Step 8: Show slide 7–5. Ask each pair of participants to share its ideas with the class.

Step 9: Write the ideas on a flipchart. (**Note to facilitator:** If themes emerge during this process, use them to organize the participants' ideas.)

9:45 Show slide 7–6. Tell the participants that the recap exercise is meant to help them capture their learning and prepare to use their new knowledge on the job.

Structured Exercise 7–2

Step 1: Ask each pair to answer the questions on the slide.

Step 2: After 10–15 minutes have each pair share its answers with the group.

Option: Ask participants to write out their answers so they can be given to their managers for follow-up after the training.

10:00 Show slide 7–7. Thank the group for its work on this module and encourage everyone to use the ideas they uncovered right away. Explain that although we cannot control the number of hours in a day, we control what we do within those hours.

What to Do Next

◆ Review Table 1–1: Sales Training Modules Matrix, to determine how best to use the module in this chapter and the type of sales personnel who would benefit from it. Also review the sales gap analyses completed by the sales personnel to identify which other modules to use with the material from this chapter. Finally, review the information in chapter 1 on how best to use this book to fit your situation.

◆ For the first few modules you facilitate, plan on one hour of preparation for every hour of facilitation. As you gain experience with the modules, plan on 20 minutes of preparation for every hour of facilitation.

- ◆ Determine how much time is available for the training session. Schedule the session. Arrange for the facility and audiovisual equipment (projector, sound system, computer). Gather the other materials you will need.

- ◆ Determine food and beverage requirements and make necessary arrangements.

- ◆ Invite participants. Send confirmation with an agenda or a list of the modules to be covered.

- ◆ Prepare copies of Training Instrument 7–1 to match your enrollment.

- ◆ Practice. Carefully review the training materials. Be prepared to respond to questions that the materials and activities are likely to generate. Review the PowerPoint presentation and practice in front of a friend or colleague to become comfortable with the key points and slide transitions and to solidify your understanding of the topic.

- ◆ As much as possible, check all arrangements in the training room the night before (if training starts in the morning) or two to three hours prior to the start of the session.

- ◆ Prepare the evaluation form (see Appendix B) for the attendees so that you can receive feedback and have information for improving the module for future training sessions.

- ◆ After the session, provide the evaluation results and any post-training assignments to the participants' managers. You also may wish to provide a summary report of any insights you obtained during the training.

◆◆◆

By now you know everything a salesperson needs to build an effective relationship and manage his or her workload appropriately. The salesforce now needs to know how to listen effectively to what the clients say and how to ask the right questions. Chapter 8 will explain all the secrets of artful listening and inquiry.

Training Instrument 7-1
Where Does My Time Go? Worksheet

ACTIVITY	IMPORTANT, URGENT	IMPORTANT, NOT URGENT	NOT IMPORTANT, URGENT	NOT IMPORTANT, NOT URGENT	ADDS VALUE

Value key: X means "yes," + adds value, = neutral, – subtracts value.

Tool 7-1

Worksheet Example: Where Does My Time Go?

ACTIVITY	IMPORTANT, URGENT	IMPORTANT, NOT URGENT	NOT IMPORTANT, URGENT	NOT IMPORTANT, NOT URGENT	ADDS VALUE
Phone calls to potential customers	X				+
Researching customers		X			+
Handling complaints	X				–
Filling out expense account forms		X			–
Entering information into CRM or SFA		X			+
Filling out reports	X				–
Colleagues visiting my workspace to chat			X		–
PR calls to existing customers		X			=
Following up on proposals/contracts	X				+
Handling service calls from customers	X				–
Eating meals	X				–
Attending sales meetings	X				=
Attending product update meetings		X			+
Answering emails/phone calls from Operations about my customers	X				–

Value key: X means "yes," + adds value, = neutral, – subtracts value.

continued on next page

Tool 7–1, condinued

Worksheet Example: Where Does My Time Go?

Notes to Facilitator

- **Phone calls to potential customers:** Important urgent and adds value—finding new business helps achieve goals. This activity could also be important not urgent, based on a salesperson's responsibilities.

- **Researching customers:** Important not urgent—this activity adds value by actually speeding up the sales cycle by reducing the amount of time with a customer at the beginning of the sales cycle or qualifying a prospect so that a sales call is not necessary.

- **Handling complaints:** Important urgent—taking care of an upset customer is very important and yet it does not add value to a salesperson's productivity. Why? If a salesperson is handling a complaint it takes away time from speaking to other customers or prospects. It is true that a dissatisfied customer who is turned around into a satisfied customer through a proper service recovery action does become loyal. However, this was existing business that was put at risk. A question for your salespeople is, what is better for overall sales productivity—sales personnel handling complaints or another department handling the call?

- **Filling out expense account forms:** Depending on the salesperson's administration abilities, this could either be important not urgent or important urgent—the activity subtracts value from productivity unless it is done during nonselling hours (when it would become neutral).

- **Entering information into customer relationship management (CRM) or sales force automation (SFA) systems:** Usually treated as important not urgent until a salesperson falls behind; then it becomes important urgent. If the activity is done while it is important urgent it adds value to productivity because it helps with planning for sales calls or developing sales strategies. If the activity is important urgent it could subtract from productivity because the salesperson would be doing this work during selling time.

- **Filling out reports:** For argument's sake consider this important urgent. This designation would make it subtract from productivity. If done outside of selling hours it would become neutral and could even add value.

- **Colleagues visiting my workspace to chat:** Not important urgent—it seems to be urgent to the colleague who stopped to chat and obviously subtracts from productivity. (However, a break every now and then is good!) A suggestion here would be to ask the salespeople how they could protect their prime selling time.

- **PR calls to existing customers** (PR for this comment means that the salesperson is calling to stay in touch and not necessarily talk about business): Important not urgent—this is a neutral activity that can set up business calls for more productivity. This activity could subtract from productivity if it is the primary type of call a salesperson uses.

continued on next page

Tool 7–1, condinued

Worksheet Example: Where Does My Time Go?

- ◆ **Following up on proposals/contracts:** It is clear that this is important urgent and adds value.

- ◆ **Handling service calls from customers:** This falls into the same category as handling complaints.

- ◆ **Eating meals:** This is included to remind everyone that there are some activities that have to be done!

- ◆ **Sales meetings:** Many salespeople might view meetings as subtracting value, and if they do, then management ought to look at what these meetings produce. My philosophy is to make sure that at worst the meeting is neutral to productivity.

- ◆ **Product update meetings:** Again this is an important not urgent activity if planned for and if the meetings add value. However, if it becomes important urgent because the salesperson procrastinated, attending such meetings could subtract from productivity.

- ◆ **Answering emails/phone calls from Operations about customers:** Important urgent because the customer's satisfaction is very important. It subtracts from value because the salesperson could spend the time talking with potential customers. For this situation the salesperson may want to look at the quality of the information about a customer and at how this information gets to the people servicing the customer.

Slide 7–1

Planning

"You've got to be very careful if you don't know where you're going, because you might not get there."

– Yogi Berra

Slide 7–2

Planning

Exercise

Where Does My Time Go? Worksheet

- Step 1 – *List all your activities for a typical week*
- Step 2 – *For each activity, make a check in one of the four boxes:*
  - *Important/Urgent*
  - *Important/Not Urgent*
  - *Not Important/Urgent*
  - *Not Important/Not Urgent*

Slide 7–3

Planning

Exercise

Where Does My Time Go? Worksheet

- Step 3 – *For each activity in the value box write in 1 of 3 symbols:*
  - + Adds Value to my productivity
  - = Neutral to my productivity
  - – Subtracts value from my productivity

Slide 7–4

Planning

Exercise

Where Does My Time Go? Worksheet

- Step 4 – *Look at the Not Important activities. Can any of these be changed or eliminated?*
- Step 5 – *Look at the Important activities that subtract value or are neutral. With your partner, come up with ideas that either eliminate the activity or reduce the time the activity takes.*

Slide 7–5

Planning

Exercise

Where Does My Time Go? Worksheet

- Step 6 – *Share your ideas with your colleagues.*

Slide 7–6

Recap

- What have you learned from this module?
- What will you use right away in your work? Why?
- How will you use what you have learned?
- What is an effective way for you to spend more time on value–added activities? Why?
- How will you know your actions are producing results?

Slide 7–7

Planning

End of the Module

Effective Listening Modules

- Two sales modules that underscore how to listen and how to ask questions

- An explanation of the three dynamics that impede effective communication

- Myriad examples of so-called word traps—words that can have multiple meanings

This chapter contains two modules that will give your salespeople the opportunity to sharpen their listening skills. Effective listening and the use of strategic questions can uncover a customer's conditions of satisfaction, concerns, and doubts, and create a mutually beneficial relationship. When a customer acknowledges a salesperson as an effective listener, the salesperson gains a competitive advantage and is well positioned to create satisfied customers.

The Artful Listening module presents the pitfalls of communication and helps salespeople examine the background of their listening. You'll review communication fundamentals and reflect on the way that customers and salespeople listen. A powerful tool for becoming an effective listener is introduced as a transition to the next module, Inquiry.

Socrates created an art form of asking questions that formed an underpinning for principles of learning. The practice of "Socratic dialogue" or inquiry became a building block for logic as taught in areas such as philosophy and law. Although salespeople don't enter a Socratic dialogue with customers, they do have significant and numerous conversations with customers. The Inquiry module shows how great questions set up effective listening, engage the customer, and help the salesperson use his or her sales mind focus to make useful decisions.

Artful Listening Module

Listening artfully is not easy! But salespeople can improve their listening skills through awareness—something this module will help create. When we listen casually, several activities go on:

- ◆ We prepare to speak, rather than listen intently.

- ◆ We distort, delete, and generalize what we hear.

- ◆ We use word traps that can create misunderstandings.

When we are aware of these activities—which occur without any effort on our part—we can improve our listening.

 Unlike the other modules in this book, this one requires you to do more talking than the participants. Therefore, facilitators tend to move quickly through the module. Do the best you can to have a rhythm that is fast enough to keep the group's attention and yet slow enough to enable the participants to absorb the material.

TRAINING OBJECTIVE

This module provides insights into effective listening and teaches how to use questions that create comfortable disclosure and a collaborative engagement with customers.

MATERIALS

- ◆ Two flipchart easels with paper and colored markers

- ◆ LCD projector, screen, and computer for running the PowerPoint presentation

- ◆ Paper for the participants to use in taking notes and during the structured exercises

- ◆ PowerPoint slides 8–1 through 8–8. Copies of the slides for this module, *Artful Listening.ppt,* are included at the end of this chapter.

CD RESOURCES

The PowerPoint presentation for this module is on the CD that accompanies this workbook. You will find more detailed instructions and help in locating files on the CD by referring to Appendix C, "Using the Compact Disc," at the back of the workbook.

SAMPLE AGENDA

9:00 a.m.   Show slide 8–1. Read the Will Rogers quote to the class: "Never miss a good chance to shut up." Sometimes the obvious is hard to do. We want to sell, and we want to satisfy our customers. Often during this process, however, we talk too much and miss the key points that our customers want to share with us. It seems like it is so natural to talk about our products or services—and it is. The mind is so fast, and it wants to share all the knowledge and skills that we have, so it's no wonder that it's hard to listen.

Table 8–1

Slide Information for the Artful Listening Module

NUMBER	TITLE/TOPIC	DESCRIPTION	TIME
8–1	Title slide: Artful listening	Lets the class get settled and lets the facilitator welcome the group as appropriate	1 minute
8–2	Listening: What's the big deal?	Prepare to speak rather than listen	1 minute
8–3	Listening: What's the big deal?	Distort—delete—generalize	1 minute
8–4	Word traps	Definition	1 minute
8–5	Word traps	Structured exercise	10–15 minutes
8–6	Am I listening to learn?	Curious—interested—great questions	1 minute
8–7	Recap	Structured exercise	10–15 minutes
8–8	End of the module		

9:05 Show slide 8–2. Tell the participants that the human brain can absorb more than 200 spoken words per minute. However, most people speak at about 100–130 words per minute. Note that the difference between what we can absorb and what we hear results in extra brain capacity. Therefore our minds can wander or prepare to talk before the customer has even finished speaking. As a result, we miss many opportunities because we miss so much of the customer's real story.

9:10 Show slide 8–3. Say that every time people communicate, three dynamics are at work. We tend to

1. distort what we hear based on our biases, fears, and desires

2. delete what we don't want to deal with

3. generalize based on our previous experiences.

Let the participants know that these three actions make communication between people difficult, even between those who want to communicate effectively. Effective communication is an act that salespeople cannot take for granted. Awareness of the tendency to filter listening is the first step toward mitigating these unintended negative effects.

Preparation for every conversation will help salespeople stay present during interactions so that they can pick up subtle cues that they ordinarily might miss.

9:15 Show slide 8–4. Tell the participants that another pitfall to listening and communicating are so-called word traps—using words that have many possible interpretations or allowing customers to use them without asking for clarification. This practice can lead to a dangerous trap of misunderstanding.

Descriptors such as "great" or "busy," which have no standards, are a trap. If your client desires a "great" location, clarify: "What would make this location great for you?" When we listen, it's important to seek understanding of the definitions and standards that apply to potential word traps.

9:30   Show slide 8–5. Ask the group to identify the word traps on the slide.

- This is an *easy* sale.

- She is a *tough* client.

- You *really like* the product.

- My boss *doesn't understand*.

- This is a *big* account.

Each of the italicized words above is a word trap that may have different meanings to different people. Tell participants that now they're going to work on the word traps that they often use and that could create misunderstandings with their customers.

Structured Exercise 8–1

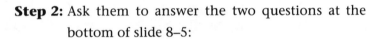

Step 1: Split the group into pairs.

Step 2: Ask them to answer the two questions at the bottom of slide 8–5:

- What are your favorite word traps? (words or phrases a salesperson often uses)

- What are your customers' favorite word traps? (words or phrases that salespeople often hear)

Step 3: After five minutes ask the pairs to share their word traps and their customers' word traps with the rest of the group.

Step 4: Ask the pairs to develop different words or phrases that are specific and that can replace the word traps. Allow 10 minutes.

Step 5: Ask the pairs to share their work with the group.

Step 6: You may want to write down the new phrases and words so that you can share the list with participants after the training.

9:45   Show slide 8–6. Go over the following key points:

◆ We have learned that we often prepare to speak rather than listen intently.

◆ We all distort, delete, and generalize when we listen, and word traps are everywhere in our conversations.

Ask the participants the following question: "Given these challenges, how do we listen artfully?" Say that they must ask the powerful question, "Am I listening to learn?" Note that this question immediately improves listening and allows the listener to use the three important characteristics of artful listening noted on slide 8–6:

1. **Curious.** When we are curious we learn and we want to listen.

2. **Interested.** Being interested helps our concentration and focus.

3. **Great questions.** Asking great questions improves our listening, as well as the customer's listening.

9:50   Show slide 8–7. Note that the following exercise will help salespeople capture their learning and prepare to use their new knowledge on the job.

Structured Exercise 8–2

Step 1: Ask each pair to answer the questions on slide 8–7. Allow 10–15 minutes.

Step 2: Ask each pair to share its answers with the group.

Option: Ask the participants to write out their answers so they can be given to their managers for follow-up after the training.

10:15   Show slide 8–8. Being an artful listener is very important to being a successful salesperson and requires awareness of how the mind works. We cannot turn down the capacity of our brain, but we can be aware of how we listen and of the words we use. This reflective thinking leads to becoming an artful listener and often creates satisfied customers.

Inquiry Module

Asking great questions is key to relationship building and helping customers move through a sales cycle. Developing a repertoire of great questions helps the salesperson become a facilitator of this process, and skillful inquiry is an art that each person can learn. The magic of artful inquiry resides in the quality of our listening because listening is the key to a client's comfortably disclosing her or his needs, desires, and conditions of satisfaction.

Inquiry, when used effectively, reveals the customer's conditions of satisfaction. These conditions are explicit and implicit—with the latter being more important. The implicit conditions of satisfaction are most often the emotional reasons for purchasing a product or service, and thus they become key decision drivers. Artful inquiry seeks to make the customer's implicit conditions of satisfaction explicit and to lead to higher levels of customer satisfaction. If the salesperson doesn't uncover these conditions, the customer can begin to doubt the salesperson, the organization, or both. These concerns, when hidden, can come up toward the end of the sales cycle and cause the salesperson to lose the business or to spend time saving the business. Both are a waste of the salesperson's most perishable resource—time.

The participants in this training module will need to have taken the conditions of satisfaction module or be experienced salespeople who are familiar with the concept of conditions of satisfaction. This module is not recommended for individual training, but you can present this module to a mix of new and experienced salespeople, if desired.

TRAINING OBJECTIVE

This module will improve the inquiry skills of the participants so that they can get their customers to disclose important information, such as implicit conditions of satisfaction.

KEY POINTS IN THIS MODULE

- ♦ Inquiry sets up listening.

- ♦ Effective inquiry helps build a relationship with customers and makes it comfortable for them to disclose information.

- ♦ Uncovering implicit conditions of satisfaction is important for customer satisfaction.

MATERIALS

- Two flipchart easels with paper and colored markers

- LCD projector, screen, and computer for running the PowerPoint presentation

- Paper for the participants to use in taking notes and during the structured exercises

- Tool 8–1: Qualification Questions (All tools for this module are located at the end of this chapter and on the CD.)

- Tool 8–2: Understanding the Customer Questions

- Tool 8–3: Conditions of Satisfaction Questions

- Tool 8–4: Asking for the Business Questions

- PowerPoint slides 8–9 through 8–29. Copies of the slides for this module, *Inquiry.ppt,* are included at the end of this chapter.

Note to facilitator: Tools 8–1 through 8–4 are provided for your use in preparing for the structured exercises in this module. The tools can also be handed out to participants when the exercises are complete.

CD RESOURCES

Materials for this module appear both in this workbook and as electronic files on the CD that accompanies the book. To access the files, insert the CD and look at its "PDF Files" directory for the tools needed. The PowerPoint presentation is also on the CD. You will find more detailed instructions and help in locating files on the CD by referring to Appendix C, "Using the Compact Disc," at the back of the workbook.

SAMPLE AGENDA

9:00 a.m.   Show slide 8–9. Read the quote to the audience—"Make it easy for a customer to talk with you." Let the participants know that effective questions lead to comfortable disclosure by the customer. It is through comfortable disclosure that customers will find it easy to talk with you. In this module, the participants will learn how to design effective questions. They also can use what they learned in the Tasks and Relationships module in chapter 5 to

Table 8–2

Slide Information for the Inquiry Module

NUMBER	TITLE/TOPIC	DESCRIPTION	TIME
8–9	Title slide: Inquiry	Lets the class get settled and lets the facilitator welcome the group as appropriate	1 minute
8–10	Definition	Definition of inquiry	1 minute
8–11	The basics	Closed-ended questions	1 minute
8–12	The basics	Open-ended questions	1 minute
8–13	The basics	Structured exercise	5 minutes
8–14	Linking questions	An explanation	1 minute
8–15	Linking questions	Pointers for linking questions	1 minute
8–16	Practice	Structured exercise	5–10 minutes
8–17	Sales cycle and questions	Different questions for different phases	1 minute
8–18	Crafting questions	Formula for crafting questions	1 minute
8–19	Qualification questions	Discussion question	2–3 minutes
8–20	Practice	Structured exercise	5–10 minutes
8–21	Understanding the customer questions	Discussion question	2–3 minutes
8–22	Practice	Structured exercise	5–10 minutes
8–23	Conditions of satisfaction review	Implicit and explicit	1 minute
8–24	Conditions of satisfaction review	Discussion question	2–3 minutes
8–25	Practice	Structured exercise	5–10 minutes
8–26	Practice	Structured exercise	5–10 minutes
8–27	Practice	Structured exercise	5–10 minutes
8–28	Recap	Structured exercise	10–15 minutes
8–29	End of the module		

further tune their questions—especially the timing of the questions.

9:05   Show slide 8–10. Say that this definition of inquiry is presented to gain a common understanding about what the word "inquiry" means.

Asking great questions is another key to great relationship building and helping customers move through a sales cycle. Developing a repertoire of great questions supports the salesperson as a facilitator of this process.

Skillful inquiry is an art that each of us can learn. The magic of artful inquiry resides in the quality of our listening—listening is the key to our clients feeling comfortable in disclosing their needs, desires, and conditions of satisfaction.

Inquiry, when used effectively, reveals the customer's conditions of satisfaction.

Refresher on Conditions of Satisfaction

These conditions are explicit and implicit, with the latter being more important. The implicit conditions of satisfaction are most often the emotional reasons for purchasing a product or service, and thus are key drivers for a decision to buy or not buy.

Artful inquiry seeks to make the customer's implicit conditions of satisfaction explicit and to lead to higher levels of customer satisfaction. If these conditions are not uncovered, the customer can begin to have doubts and concerns about the salesperson or the organization. These doubts and concerns, when hidden, can come up toward the end of the sales cycle and cause the salesperson to lose the business or to spend more time saving the business. Either outcome is a waste of the salesperson's most perishable resource—time.

9:10   Show slide 8–11. Remind the participants that there are two basic forms of questions: closed-ended questions and open-ended questions.

Closed-ended questions result in brief answers of one or two words or a short phrase. Each question on the slide is a closed-ended one and calls for simple answers like 10 a.m., yes, no, or five.

Ask the group to give you some examples of closed-ended questions other than those on the slide.

Show slide 8–12. Teach the participants that open-ended questions are the opposite of closed-ended one. These questions prompt the listener to think about the answer and provide a narrative response. A great open-ended question creatively invites the respondent to describe, expand, and embellish, and it appeals to the head and the heart. These kinds of questions help build alignment and thus the relationship.

Ask the group to give you some examples of open-ended questions other than those on the slide.

9:15 Show slide 8–13 and have the participants work on the questions noted on the slide in the structured exercise below.

Structured Exercise 8–3

Step 1: Split the group into pairs or trios.

Step 2: Ask them to answer the two questions on the slide:

1. When do you use closed-ended questions?

2. When do you use open-ended questions?

Step 3: After three to five minutes, ask the pairs or trios to share their ideas with the group.

Potential answers for closed-ended questions include

♦ to control a conversation that is no longer focused (for example, Is it okay if we get back to talking about the technical specification?)

- to confirm an understanding (for example, Now that we have reached this point, is it time to submit a proposal?)

- to ask permission (for example, May I ask you a few questions? Is this a good time to talk about *x*?)

- to qualify a customer (for example, Do you purchase products/services similar to ours?).

Potential answers for open-ended questions include

- to learn what the customer thinks about a product or service (for example, How would you rate our product and why?)

- to qualify a customer (for example, Who do you like to work with? What do you know about our product or services?)

- to understand the customer and his or her organization (for example, What are your key strategies?)

- to uncover why a customer will buy (for example, What are the key elements in the product/service you are seeking?).

- to ask for the business. (For example, What will it take to get your business?)

 9:25 Show slide 8–14. Tell the participants that linking questions allow a conversation to move in a systematic path, using the answer to one question to spur the next question. Explain that this is a uniquely effective way to gather new information and insight for the salesperson and the client.

The questions that provoke the most revealing responses tend to grow from the continuation of the story that is unfolding within the conversation.

9:30 Show slide 8–15. Say this is a technique that requires thinking on one's feet. Here are a few pointers to share with the participants:

- ◆ Be ready for opportunities. Listen attentively to the client's responses to your questions, and you'll find opportunities to ask a linking question that will lead to productive territory.

- ◆ The point is to gain a deeper understanding of the client's desires and aspirations.

- ◆ Be curious. Open-ended questions work best. Ask "why," "how," and "what" questions.

- ◆ Linking three to five questions often leads to understanding the client's true concerns and implicit conditions of satisfaction.

- ◆ Manage the conversation and the time. Linking questions take time, so manage them within the context of the entire conversation and the known time constraints.

- ◆ Know when to stop. By being prepared for the conversation and paying close attention to the richness of the responses, you should intuitively know when to move off a particular chain of questions.

9:35 Show slide 8–16 and have participants work on the questions noted there in the structured exercise below.

Structured Exercise 8–4

Step 1: Split the group into pairs.

Step 2: Explain that the exercise is for partners to learn something about each other that they don't already know by linking open-ended questions.

Step 3: Instruct partner A to ask an open-ended question of partner B, and then ask five to six more open-ended questions that are each linked to the answer of the previous question.

Step 4: Instruct partner B to give feedback about the linking of questions and whether open-ended questions were used.

Step 5: Have pairs switch roles and repeat steps 3 and 4.

Step 6: Ask pairs to share with the group what they learned about linking questions.

9:50   Show slide 8–17. Say that for the purposes of this training module, you will use a simple four-phase sales cycle to categorize questions:

1. **Qualification:** qualify the customer to determine if you should continue

2. **Understanding the customer:** learn about the customer, the organization, and the industry to uncover needs, opportunities, and the customer's style

3. **Conditions of satisfaction:** identify conditions of satisfaction to develop a compelling offer that differentiates from the competition

4. **Agreement:** reach agreement (this phase will be covered in the module on compelling offers).

Ask participants if they would agree to those terms. If your organization already has a defined sales cycle, you may wish to use your own terms.

9:55   Show slide 8–18. Tell the participants that the following simple model for crafting great questions can be used to create questions for each phase of the sales cycle:

◆ *Desired outcome:* First, know exactly what information you are after and define it as specifically as possible. Write it down so you (and others, if you are working with a team) can look at it.

◆ *Intention:* Think about why you are trying to get this particular information. What's the point and where will it lead?

◆ *Open-ended and closed-ended questions:* If you want to elicit a big response, be sure to craft an open-ended question that creatively invites the respondent to describe, expand, and embellish, and appeals to the head and the heart. These kinds of questions help build alignment and thus the relationship.

◆ *Unintended consequences:* Explore any unintended consequences the question might trigger. For example, asking too many open-ended questions in an initial meeting might irritate the customer.

10:10   Show slide 8–19. Ask the group, "What do we need to know about a prospect or new customer to go forward in the sales process?" (**Note to facilitator:** Write the responses on a flipchart.)

10:20   Show slide 8–20 and have the participants work on the structured exercise below.

Structured Exercise 8–5

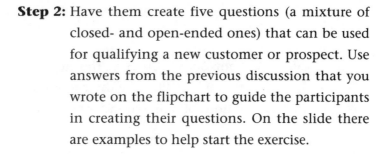

Step 1: Split the group into pairs or trios.

Step 2: Have them create five questions (a mixture of closed- and open-ended ones) that can be used for qualifying a new customer or prospect. Use answers from the previous discussion that you wrote on the flipchart to guide the participants in creating their questions. On the slide there are examples to help start the exercise.

Step 3: After 5–10 minutes have each pair or trio share its five questions.

Step 4: Write the questions on a flipchart. (The questions can be used for training follow-up.)

10:30   Show slide 8–21. Ask the group, "What do we need to know about a customer to uncover needs, opportunities, and his or her style?" Write the responses on a flipchart.

10:35   Show slide 8–22 and have the participants work on the following structured exercise.

Structured Exercise 8–6

Step 1: Split the group into pairs or trios.

Step 2: Have each pair or trio create five questions (a mixture of closed- and open-ended questions) that can be used for understanding the customer. Use answers from the previous discussion that you wrote on the flipchart to guide the participants in creating their questions. On the slide there are examples to help start the exercise.

Step 3: After 5–10 minutes have each pair or trio share its five questions and write the questions on the flipchart. (The questions can be used for training follow-up.)

10:45   Show slide 8–23. Review the definitions of implicit and explicit conditions of satisfaction:

◆ implicit: capable of being understood from something not expressed, revealed, or developed

◆ explicit: fully revealed or expressed without vagueness, implication, or ambiguity; leaves no question as to meaning or intent.

10:50   Show slide 8–24. Have the group answer the question on the slide: "What are the major implicit and explicit conditions of satisfaction for your customers?"

Option: You can use the flipcharts created in the Conditions of Satisfaction module to supplement this group discussion.

10:55   Show slide 8–25 and have the participants work on the questions in the structured exercise below.

Structured Exercise 8–7

Step 1: Split the group into pairs or trios.

Step 2: Have them create five questions (a mixture of closed- and open-ended ones) that can be used for uncovering explicit conditions of satisfaction.

Use answers from the previous discussion that you wrote on the flipchart to guide the participants in creating their questions. On the slide there are examples to help start the exercise.

Step 3: After 10–15 minutes have each pair or trio share its five questions.

Step 4: Write the questions on the flipchart. (The questions can be used for training follow-up.)

11:10   Show slide 8–26 and have the participants work on the questions in the structured exercise below.

Structured Exercise 8–8

Step 1: Split the group into pairs or trios.

Step 2: Have them create five questions (a mixture of close and open ended questions) that can be used for uncovering implicit conditions of satisfaction. Use answers from the previous discussion that you wrote on the flipchart to guide the participants in creating their questions. On the slide there are examples to help start the exercise.

Step 3: After 10–15 minutes have each pair or trio share its five questions.

Step 4: Write the questions on the flipchart. (The questions can be used for training follow-up.)

11:25   Show slide 8–27. Tell the participants that sometimes, even when using effective inquiry skills, the salesperson's human radar tells her or him that the client needs some more information to make a decision. If many questions already have been asked, more questions might be counterproductive to the relationship. This is where a "nonquestion" can help. On the slide are several examples of nonquestions that inquire:

◆   *You may be wondering . . .*

◆   *Many people ask me . . .*

- *Maybe we need to talk about . . .*

- *Perhaps you're wondering . . .*

Structured Exercise 8–9

Step 1: Split the group into pairs or trios.

Step 2: Have them finish the sentences on the slide and create one or two more examples of this tool.

Step 3: Ask them the two questions on the slide. (When would you use this tool? Why?).

Step 4: After 5–10 minutes have each pair or trio share its five questions.

Step 5: Write the questions on the flipchart. (The questions can be used for training follow-up.)

11:40   Show slide 8–28. Tell the participants that the following exercise will help them capture their learning and prepare to use their new knowledge on the job.

Structured Exercise 8–10

Step 1: Split the groups into pairs.

Step 2: Ask each pair to answer the questions on the slide.

Step 3: After 10–15 minutes have each pair share its answers with the group.

Option: Ask the participants to write out their answers so they can be given to their managers for follow-up after the training.

Noon   Show slide 8–29. Ask each participant to share one new question he or she has discovered and when it will be used. After everyone has responded, thank everyone for participating in the training.

What To Do Next

◆ Review Table 1–1: Sales Training Modules Matrix for help in determining how best to use the module in this chapter and the type of sales personnel who would benefit. Also review the matrix and the sales gap analyses completed by the sales personnel to determine which other modules you might want to use. Finally, review the information in chapter 1 on how best to use this book to fit your situation.

◆ For the first few modules you facilitate, plan on one hour of preparation for every hour of facilitation. As you gain experience with the modules, plan on 20 minutes of preparation for every hour of facilitation.

◆ Determine how much time is available for the training session. Schedule the session. Arrange for the facility and audiovisual equipment (projector, screen, sound system, and computer). Gather the other materials you will need.

◆ Determine food and beverage requirements and make necessary arrangements.

◆ Invite participants. Send confirmation with an agenda or a list of the modules to be covered.

◆ Prepare copies of training materials to match your enrollment.

◆ Practice. Carefully review the training materials. Be prepared to respond to questions that the materials and activities are likely to generate. Review the PowerPoint presentation and practice in front of a friend or colleague so you're comfortable with the key points and slide transitions and have a solid understanding of the topic.

◆ Based on the number of participants, determine how you will conduct the structured exercises (in pairs or trios) and the method you will use for splitting the class into working groups (for example, counting off, letting each person choose a partner, and so forth).

◆ As much as possible, check all arrangements in the training room the night before (when training starts in the morning), or two to three hours prior to the start of the session.

◆ Prepare the evaluation form (see Appendix B) for the attendees so that you can receive feedback and have information for improving the modules for future training sessions.

◆ After the session, provide the evaluation results and any post-training assignments to the participants' managers. You also may wish to provide a summary report of any insights you obtained during the training.

◆ ◆ ◆

Now that your salespeople know how to listen and how to ask the right questions, it's time for them to use those skills. Now they need a formula for effective communication—something you'll find in the next chapter. Also in chapter 9: guidelines for effective email—something that plagues even the best salesperson.

Tool 8–1

Qualification Questions

- Do you purchase products similar to ours?

- How much product/service do you purchase in a year?

- How many suppliers do you use?

- How often do you switch suppliers?

- What are the criteria for switching?

- Who do you like to work with? (helps uncover competitors)

- Have you heard about our company or products?

- What is your opinion of our product/service?

- What led you to contact us?

- How did you learn about our product/service?

- How important is this product/service to your business?

- What information do you have about our product/service?

- What and how much information are you seeking about our product/service?

- What experience have you had with similar products/services?

- Are you considering selecting new suppliers?

- What piques your interest in us?

- How are purchase decisions made at your company?

Tool 8–2
Understanding the Customer Questions

- What are your goals for this year?

- How would you prioritize those goals?

- What has to go right to meet or exceed those goals?

- Are you achieving your goals?

- In your opinion, what obstacles keep you from achieving your goals?

- What key strategies are you responsible for implementing?

- What are your industry's hot buttons?

- How are the industry trends affecting you?

- How do you segment your customers?

- How is your company organized?

- What is working in your current situation?

- What is not working in your current situation?

- What are your criteria for success?

- How do you evaluate vendors/suppliers?

- What causes your company problems on a daily basis? Your department? You?

- How would you describe your responsibilities?

- What are your customers asking of you?

- What is your greatest challenge?

- What new products are you developing?

- What is your typical decision-making process?

Tool 8–3

Conditions of Satisfaction Questions

◆ What piqued your interest in our product/service?

◆ What has been your experience with x [a competitor]?

◆ What are some of the ways you would use our product/service?

◆ What are the key elements in the product/service you are seeking?

◆ What are the main reasons for using x's product/services?

◆ What are your expectations of x's product/service?

◆ What do you like most and least in dealing with suppliers?

◆ Do you have a list of specifics that you need?

◆ Do you have technical specifications?

◆ What are your standards for satisfaction?

◆ Are you pleased with your current situation? Why?

◆ Describe your ideal suppler.

◆ Who are your best suppliers and what do they provide that makes them the best?

◆ What do you not get from x that would make a significant impact if you could get it?

◆ Outside of price, what other considerations are important?

◆ What product performance issues are you trying to address?

◆ If you had your wish, what would be the perfect product/service?

◆ What frustrates you about x's product/service, and why?

◆ How do you rate the quality of x's product/service?

◆ What does x do that we do not do?

◆ What buying criteria are important to you?

◆ Can you tell me more about your thinking?

◆ Is there a format that you prefer for . . . [billing, communication, planning]?

◆ How much time do you have to make this decision?

◆ Do you like big picture before small picture, or do you prefer to get all the details first?

◆ How are your procurement efforts evaluated?

◆ How can we organize our proposal for you so that it is easy for you to compare our offers with other offers you receive?

Tool 8–4

Asking for the Business Questions

- Are there any open issues to review before we present our proposal or contract?

- Have we forgotten anything?

- Is there anything else I need to know for our proposal/contract?

- Does that sound okay to you?

- Is the next step to send a proposal/contract?

- What is the best way to proceed?

- Should I send a draft proposal/contract to you first for review?

- What do we need to provide you so that we can send a proposal/contract?

- What do you think about our offer?

- Does our offer make sense?

- Do we understand your situation well enough to submit a proposal?

- How much time would you like to review our offer and provide feedback so we can finalize a contract?

- What will it take to get your business?

- What is the best way to present our offer to you?

- How many copies of the proposal shall we provide?

- May I submit a proposal to you [tomorrow, next week . . .]?

Slide 8–1

Artful Listening

"Never miss a good chance to shut up."
– Will Rogers

Slide 8–2

Artful Listening

Listening – What's the Big Deal?

You are literally biologically wired not to listen.

Overcapacity...

We prepare to speak rather than listen...

Slide 8–3

Artful Listening

Listening – What's the Big Deal?

Distort

Delete

Generalize

Slide 8–4

Artful Listening

Word Traps

Common words and phrases that have different meanings to different people and yet are spoken as if there is a universal understanding.

Slide 8–5

Artful Listening

Where are the word traps?

- This is an easy sale.
- She is a tough client.
- You really like the product.
- My boss doesn't understand.
- This is a big account.

What are your favorite word traps?
What are your customer's favorite word traps?

Slide 8–6

Artful Listening

Am I Listening to Learn?

- Curious
- Interested
- Great questions

Slide 8–7

Recap

- What have you learned from this module?
- What will you use right away in your work? Why?
- How will you use what you have learned?
- What is an effective way for you to actively improve your listening? Why?
- How will you know your actions are producing results?

Slide 8–8

Artful Listening

End of the Module

Slide 8–9

Inquiry

"Make it easy for a customer to talk with you."
– Harvey Mackay

Slide 8–10

Inquiry

Definition

Examination into facts or principles, a request for information

Slide 8–11

Inquiry

The Basics

- **Closed-ended questions – ones that result in short answers:**
  - *What time is it?*
  - *Did you like the proposal?*
  - *Would you like me to call next week?*
  - *Did we meet your technical specifications?*
  - *Is this a good time to talk with you?*
  - *How many copies shall I prepare?*

Slide 8–12

Inquiry

The Basics

- **Open-ended questions – ones that prompt the listener to provide thoughtful or narrative-type answers:**
  - *What is working about your current situation?*
  - *What kind of a year are you having?*
  - *What worked with your last project?*
  - *How would you describe your responsibilities?*
  - *How would you rate our product, and why?*

Slide 8–13

Inquiry

- When do you use closed–ended questions?

- When do you use open–ended questions?

Slide 8–14

Inquiry

Linking Questions

Moving in a systematic path, using the answer to one question to spur the next question is a uniquely effective way to gather new information and insight for both you and your customers.

Slide 8–15

Inquiry

Linking Questions

- Be ready for opportunities
- Be in the mood of curiosity
- Link 3–5 questions
- Manage the conversation and the time
- Know when to stop

Slide 8–16

Practice

With a partner practice linking questions:

- Partner A will ask an opening question of partner B *(the purpose is to learn something about your partner that you don't already know)*, and then ask 5–6 more open–ended questions.
- Partner B gives feedback about the linking of questions and if open–ended questions were used.
- Switch partners and repeat Steps 1 and 2.
- Partners share with the group what they learned about linking questions.

Slide 8–17

Inquiry

Sales Cycle and Questions

- A typical sales cycle has four phases that require different questions:
  1. Qualification
  2. Understanding the customer, their organization, their industry and customers
  3. Conditions of satisfaction
  4. Agreement

Slide 8–18

Inquiry

Crafting Questions

- Desired outcome
- Intention
- Open–ended or closed–ended question
- Unintended consequences

TIP: Craft questions to start linking questions for the purpose of going 4–5 levels deep.

Slide 8–19

Inquiry

Qualification Questions

What do we need to know about a prospect or a new customer to go forward in the sales process?

Slide 8–20

Practice

Create five questions that you can use for qualifying a new customer or prospect.

- What closed–ended questions will help you with qualification?
  - *Example:* Have you ever considered purchasing this type of product before?
- What open–ended questions will help you with qualification?
  - *Example:* What is your process for considering a new supplier?

Slide 8–21

Qualification Questions

Understanding the Customer Questions

What do we need to know about a customer to uncover needs, opportunities, and their style?

Slide 8–22

Practice

- Select 1–2 customers.
- Create five questions for understanding the customer that you can use for your next call.
  - What closed–ended questions would you use?
    - *Example:* Are you achieving your goals?
  - What open–ended questions would you use?
    - *Example:* In your opinion, what obstacles keep you from achieving your goals?

Slide 8–23

Inquiry

Implicit and Explicit Conditions of Satisfaction

- Implicit – Capable of being understood from something else, though not expressed or involved in the nature or essence of something; not revealed, expressed, or developed
- Explicit – Fully revealed or expressed without vagueness, implication, or ambiguity; leaving no question as to meaning or intent

Slide 8–24

Inquiry

Implicit and Explicit Conditions of Satisfaction

- What are the major implicit and explicit conditions of satisfaction for your customers?

Slide 8–25

Practice

- Select 1–2 customers.
- Create five questions for uncovering explicit conditions of satisfaction that you can use for your next call.
  - What closed–ended questions would you use to uncover explicit conditions of satisfaction?
    - *Example: Do you have technical specifications?*
  - What open–ended questions would you use to uncover explicit conditions of satisfaction?
    - *Example: What are your standards for satisfaction?*

Slide 8–26

Practice

- Select 1–2 customers.
- Create five questions for uncovering implicit conditions of satisfaction that you can use for your next call.
  - What closed–ended questions would you use to uncover implicit conditions of satisfaction?
    - *Example: Shall I copy you on all my email messages?*
  - What open–ended questions would you use to uncover implicit conditions of satisfaction?
    - *Example: How is your performance measured?*

Slide 8–27

Inquiry
Conditions of Satisfaction Questions

The non-question question
  - *You may be wondering...*
  - *Many people ask me...*
  - *Maybe we need to talk about...*
  - *Perhaps you're wondering...*

- Complete the sentences above and create 1–2 more examples.
- Then answer the following question:
  - When would you use this tool, and why?

Slide 8–28

Recap

- What have you learned from this module?
- What will you use right away in your work? Why?
- How will you use what you have learned?
- What is an effective way for you to actively improve your inquiry skills? Why?
- How will you know your actions are producing results?

Slide 8–29

Inquiry

End of the Module

Communicating: A Basic Formula Module

- ◆ A sales module that outlines a basic formula for communication

- ◆ Detailed explanations of each communication component: body language, voice tone, and words

- ◆ Guidelines for effective email, written, phone, and in-person communication

Every working day salespeople spend most of their time communicating, and often the content of the communication is highly repetitive. This repetition can lead one to communicate without thinking about the quality of his or her communication. In today's fast-paced, highly competitive market, customers expect salespeople to communicate at an exceptional level in all media—face-to-face, by telephone, and in written communication. They expect salespeople to be skillfully articulate about products, artful with inquiry, polished in their presentations, and both direct and authentic.

Many salespeople have had extensive experience and success with face-to-face communication. However, as more companies move toward Web-based marketing, the telephone and written electronic media become more dominant means of communication. So salespeople need to become more adept at communicating through those media.

Understanding the components of communication will help your salespeople use the basic formula for communicating that this module presents. The components of communication, broken down by percentage, are as follows:

- ◆ body language = 55 percent

- ◆ voice tone = 38 percent

- ◆ words = 7 percent.

On the basis of this breakdown, salespeople are using 100 percent of their capacity to communicate in a face-to-face interaction with customers. With body language literally speaking louder than words and the added dimension of tone, the salesperson can rely on her or his body and tone to overcome small mistakes in the selection of words. When communicating over the phone, voice tone is the critical component to effective communication. For written communications, salespeople have the most chance for misinterpretation because they are operating with only 7 percent of their capacity to communicate. When a salesperson understands these percentages, he or she can prepare for the type of communication that will be used.

Preparation is especially important for a frequently used method of communication—email. Easy to use and easily abused, email provides conveniences and challenges. The convenience: reaching the client directly and instantly. The challenge: misinterpreting important information. The basic formula presented in this module will help salespeople create email messages that get the desired response.

Experienced salespeople might find that the sections on in-person and telephone communications repeat what they already know. Experienced salespeople will benefit most from the section on written communications. The written communication exercise focuses on email—one of today's dominant media.

Training Objective

This module provides a formula that salespeople can use for all communications, with a special emphasis on written communications, such as email.

Key Points in This Module

- ◆ Salespeople constantly communicate in all forms, often using repetitive messages, which opens the possibility that the intended message will not be received.

- ◆ In today's market, customers expect salespeople to communicate exceptionally well in all media—face-to-face, by telephone, and in written form.

- ◆ More companies have moved toward Web-based marketing. The telephone and written electronic media dominate communication.

◆ Basic components of communication are 55 percent body language, 38 percent voice tone, and 7 percent words.

◆ Written communication, especially email, is the most challenging form of communication because it uses only 7 percent of the salesperson's ability to communicate.

◆ Learning a basic formula for communication and using it consistently will improve all forms of communication.

Materials

◆ Two flipchart easels with paper and colored markers

◆ LCD projector, screen, and computer for running the PowerPoint presentation

◆ Paper for the participants to use in taking notes

◆ PowerPoint slides 9–1 through 9–16. Copies of the slides for this module, *Basic Formula.ppt,* are included at the end of this chapter.

◆ Training Instrument 9–1: Worksheet: Communicating in Person

◆ Tool 9–1: Worksheet Example: Communicating in Person

◆ Training Instrument 9–2: Worksheet: Communicating by Telephone

◆ Tool 9–2: Worksheet Example: Communicating by Telephone

◆ Training Instrument 9–3: Worksheet: Communicating in Writing by Letter, Email, or Fax

◆ Tool 9–3 Worksheet: Communicating in Writing by Email

◆ Brochures and other marketing collateral items that your organization uses

◆ List of key marketing messages that your organization uses

CD Resources

Materials for this module appear both in this workbook and as electronic files on the CD that accompanies the book. To access the files, insert the CD and look at its "PDF Files" directory for the training instruments and tools needed. The PowerPoint presentation is also on the CD. You will find more detailed instructions and help in locating files on the CD by referring to Appendix C, "Using the Compact Disc," at the back of the workbook.

Sample Agenda

9:00 a.m.	Show slide 9–1. Mark Twain must have been clairvoyant about email when he wrote this statement: "I didn't have time to write a short letter, so I wrote a long one instead."

Sometimes it seems easier to write a long email than a short one. Shorter email can be difficult because there are several key points to cover. This leads to quite a dilemma. If the communication is too long the customer may not read it all, and if it is too short the customer might misinterpret or not fully understand what you are trying to communicate. This module uses a basic formula to help you with this dilemma—especially with email messages.

9:05   Show slide 9–2. Tell your audience that when we communicate, we use one, two, or three of the communication components. Some components are more powerful than others, as shown on the slide:

- body language = 55 percent

- voice tone = 38 percent

- words = 7 percent.

9:10   Show slide 9–3. Tell the participants that when we are face-to-face with a customer, we use 100 percent of our capacity to communicate, and our body language speaks louder than words or voice tone. A customer's human radar can really tune in to body language.

On the phone it is voice tone that is the most important aspect. If a mistake is made with words, voice tone can sometimes overcome the mistake.

Written communication, because it relies only on words, uses your lowest capacity to communicate and offers the greatest opportunity for miscommunication. In this

Table 9–1

Slide Information for the Communicating: A Basic Formula Module

NUMBER	TITLE/TOPIC	DESCRIPTION	TIME
9–1	Title slide: Communicating— a basic formula	Enables the class to get settled and the facilitator to welcome the group as appropriate	1 minute
9–2	The components	Body language, tone, and words	1 minute
9–3	Communicating	Face-to-face, telephone, and written communication	1 minute
9–4	Basic formula	Four steps	1 minute
9–5	Preparation	Four questions	1 minute
9–6	Draft the message	Framework	1 minute
9–7	Check for unintended consequences	Two questions	1 minute
9–8	Refine	Two discussion questions	2–3 minutes
9–9	Applying the model	In-person communication	1 minute
9–10	Face-to-face	Structured exercise	10–15 minutes
9–11	Applying the model	Telephone communication	1 minute
9–12	Telephone	Structured exercise	10–15 minutes
9–13	Applying the model	Written communication	1 minute
9–14	Written communication (email)	Structured exercise	15–20 minutes
9–15	Recap	Structured exercise	10–15 minutes
9–16	End of the module		

module you will get a chance to work on today's most often used form of written communication—email.

9:15   Show slide 9–4. Introduce the basic communicating formula. Say that for important communications, whether in person or in writing, using this formula can make the participants more effective. (**Note to facilitator:** This is a transition slide and it is sufficient to just read the points on the slide and explain that you will go into detail for each point.) The basic formula is as follows:

1. prepare

2. draft the message

3. check for unintended consequences

4. refine.

9:20 Show slide 9–5. Note to the participants that preparation includes answering the questions on the slide:

◆ *What is the intention of the communication?* Effective intentions are related to either the task (selling a product or service) or the relationship with the customer. Sometimes our intentions are more selfish—such as sending an email because it's quicker, will count as a client contact, and gets an activity off our to-do list. In that case the intention is to get an activity done.

◆ *What is the essence of the message?* Here's a simple definition of essence: the most significant element, quality, or aspect of a thing or person. Thinking about the essence of a communication can help you get your message across successfully. For example, the essence of a communication might be that you want the customer to know that you are seeking to do what is best for the customer or that you listened to the customer during previous interactions.

◆ *What offer/value will you deliver to the recipient?* In a selling situation the customer wants to know what you are offering or what value you can provide. This is more than just offering a price early in the sales cycle. Sometimes the value is respecting the customer's time and making a commitment that you will not waste his or her time. Other offers might be to do research for a customer to help him or her make a decision. All effective communications offer value to the customer.

◆ *What is your request, if any?* If a request is made, make sure it is clear and has some type of a timeframe.

9:25 Show slide 9–6. Tell the participants that when the preparation is completed, a message can be drafted. Go through the bullet points on the slide. (**Note to facilitator:** In the context of this module, it is best to work on examples of written communications. However, if your salespeople use the telephone as their primary method of contact you can have them draft telephone messages or voicemail messages.)

◆ **Personalize the opening and closing:** Let the participants know that personalization helps them avoid the customer thinking that the salesperson is using standardized communications. Tell the participants that often an opening may refer to a comment made during a previous interaction or to something the salesperson has learned about the customer or their company. Say that for in-person and phone communications, referring to something in previous conversation is effective in the closing and lets the customer know that the salesperson listened to her.

◆ **Start with the big picture ... move to the details:** Tell the participants that starting with the big picture helps keep the communication focused and leads the customer through the purpose of the communication.

◆ **Present your purpose, value, or request:** Note to your participants that too often salespeople do not tell the customer why they are contacting them or do not create any value for the customer in the communication. Explain that salespeople can add value by asking a question about the customer's business that prompts the customer to reflect about the business or view it from a different perspective. Tell the participants that another way to add value is to share research information or an article that would be of interest to the customer. Of course the ultimate value is providing a product or service that helps the customer.

◆ **Recap the key points and identify the next step:** Say that recapping the key points and identifying the next step tells the customer that you listened and creates alignment about the next step.

9:30

Show slide 9–7. Tell the participants that when the message is drafted, they should check for any unintended consequences by asking two questions:

1. What are the possible consequences?

2. Are any of them negative to the task, relationship, or your organization?

A simple example might be that after reading the email draft, one might realize that because of its brevity the email does not get across the details or serious nature of the communication and a telephone call would be better for the task or relationship. Another example might be that if there is too much information to go over in a 20-minute meeting, which might make the customer feel rushed or believe she or he is being pushed into an uncomfortable timeframe, a written communication would be more appropriate and useful.

9:35

Show slide 9–8. Tell the participants that the next step in the process is refining the communication after any unintended consequences have been identified. Present the following questions, which are helpful in refining a communication:

◆ *Does the message reflect your organization's personality, tone, and manner?* Give the example of a company that is known for its friendly service and note that a standardized letter probably would not reflect the company's personality. For a professional firm, a very detailed and traditional format might best reflect the firm's personality. Ask the participants the following questions: What is our organization's personality, and what type of communication style should we use?

◆ *Have you used imagery where possible?* Tell the participants that written messages and face-to-face meetings are enhanced through pictures or images. Note that in studies of adult learning, adults remembered more when imagery was used. To explain this dynamic, use some brochures or promotional material from your company as examples. You could ask group members to explain what the images mean to them. The class might be surprised about what the images say and how much they say!

◆ *Were you able to deliver any key messages?* In many organizations the marketing department has created key messages that result from research or customer feedback. The use of these messages can be very effective in communicating with customers and reinforcing the intention of a communication.

Note to facilitator: You may want to get some of the key messages from marketing. If none are available you can use the following optional discussion questions:

◆ What are the key messages for our products or services?

◆ Is the communication aligned with the client's style and in keeping with your style?

Tell the participants that there are two dynamics in a communication—the salesperson's style and the customer's style. Give the example of a customer not interested in details but only the big picture. Tell the participants that a detail-oriented sales professional will adjust the detailed message to the needs of the customer. Another key point is that repeating sales messages exactly as presented in all other communications with the customer might make the salesperson look insincere.

9:40   Show slide 9–9. This is a transition slide to a structured exercise. Many salespeople are excellent at face-to-face interactions and therefore tend to prepare less for this type of interaction. Note that customers have individual characteristics, pace, and style. Say that in-person communication is a golden opportunity to blend your natural people skills with a disciplined approach to moving the client through the process.

9:45 Show slide 9–10. The purpose of this exercise is to provide an opportunity for experienced salespeople to refine their face-to-face communication skills and for new salespeople to develop their face-to-face communication skills.

Structured Exercise 9–1

Step 1: The exercise starts with each salesperson in the class working independently on one to two customers with whom he or she will have a face-to-face meeting in the next five to seven days. Hand out copies of the Communicating in Person worksheet (Training Instrument 9–1) and the completed example (Tool 9–1).

Ask participants to use the worksheet, stopping at step 3, to prepare for the upcoming meetings. Give them five minutes.

Step 2: When the group is ready, have participants pair up and work together on refining their communications. (**Note to facilitator:** Invite them to use questions they developed in the Inquiry module, chapter 8.) Give 5–10 minutes.

Step 3: Have them share their messages and what they learned.

Step 4: Write the messages on a flipchart. (The messages can be used for training follow-up.)

10:00 Show slide 9–11. Say that we tend to pick up the phone rather impulsively and sometimes find ourselves struggling to keep the conversation on track. As with written communication, effective telephone interactions are planned. Preparation generates positive outcomes. Note that every conversation has a flow, and the more one can plan and manage the flow, the better the outcome will be. Thinking of your intention and objectives for the call, make a list of every item you wish to cover, including an effective greeting and closing.

As is true for a great musician, practicing before the live event allows for more effective and harmonious improvisation when going live.

10:05 Show slide 9–12, which outlines the following structured exercise.

Structured Exercise 9–2

Step 1: The exercise starts with each salesperson in the class working independently on one or two customers with whom they will have an important telephone conversation in the next five to seven days. Give the participants copies of Training Instrument 9–2: Worksheet: Communicating by Telephone and the completed example (Tool 9–2). Ask them to use the worksheet, stopping at step 3, and prepare for the upcoming phone calls. (**Note to facilitator:** Invite them to use questions they developed in the Inquiry module, chapter 8.) Give them five minutes for this activity.

Step 2: When participants are ready have them pair up and work together on refining their communications. Give them 5–10 minutes.

Step 3: Have them share their messages and what they learned.

Step 4: Write the messages on a flipchart. (The messages can be used for training follow-up.)

10:20 Show slide 9–13. Tell participants that although the world seems to be shrinking because of our connectedness through technology, what is growing is the challenge of communicating in a virtual world. Less than 100 years ago, long-distance travel was a challenge and many people relied on letters for communication. Perhaps participants have read letters such as those written by Lewis and Clark or even by their own grandparents. The ability to create mental pictures and communicate complicated thoughts and feelings in writing was essential to the correspondents' relationships. With the proliferation of email as a major medium of communication, this is once again true.

Explain that written communication is unforgiving because

◆ We don't have the advantage of tone of voice, body language, or surroundings. We have only 7 percent (the words we use) of our ability to communicate.

◆ It is "permanent."

◆ People know it is not thinking out loud, like an oral conversation—the writer always controls the time allowed for consideration of what is being communicated and how it is said.

◆ Customers expect more polish and often formality in written communication.

◆ Email is particularly unforgiving because we do it quickly, thus creating opportunities for error in explicit language and implicit tone.

Although email can be interactive and affords some opportunity to ask for clarification (unlike "snail mail"), if one unintentionally offends the recipient, one may never get an opening to restate the message.

We must be especially disciplined in our approach to written communication. The guidelines given for effective communication—preparing, drafting the message, checking for unintended consequences, and refining—are doubly important here.

One way that salespeople can make their job easier is to work hard at creating some refined sentences and paragraphs that they can use, appropriately, over and over again. These might be responses to common inquiries, descriptions of general benefits, or a series of best questions they have developed.

10:25 Show slide 9–14, which outlines the following structured exercise.

Structured Exercise 9–3

Step 1: The exercise starts with each salesperson in the class working independently on one or two customers to whom they will send an email message in the next five to seven days. Distribute copies of Training Instrument 9–3 and Tool 9–3.

Ask participants to use the worksheet, stopping at step 3, and draft the email message. (**Note to facilitator:** Invite them to use questions they developed in the Inquiry module, chapter 8, if appropriate.) Give them 5–10 minutes.

Step 2: When participants are ready have them pair up and work together on refining their email message. Give them 5–10 minutes.

Step 3: Have them share their messages and what they learned.

Step 4: Write the messages on a flipchart. (The messages can be used for training follow-up.)

10:45 Show slide 9–15. Tell the participants that this exercise will help them capture their learning and prepare to use their new knowledge on the job.

Structured Exercise 9–4

Ask each pair to answer the questions on the slide. After 10–15 minutes have the pairs share their answers with the group.

Option: Ask the participants to write out their answers so they can be given to their managers for follow-up after the training.

11:00 Show slide 9–16. Thank the participants for working on this important topic and encourage them to use what they have learned right away so that they can continue to improve their communications.

What To Do Next

- Review Table 1–1: Sales Training Modules Matrix for help in determining how best to use the module in this chapter and the type of sales personnel who would benefit. Also review the matrix and the sales gap analyses completed by the sales personnel to determine which other modules you might want to use. Finally, review the information in chapter 1 on how best to use this book to fit your situation.

- For the first few modules you facilitate, plan on one hour of preparation for every hour of facilitation. As you gain experience with the modules, plan on 20 minutes of preparation for every hour of facilitation.

- Determine the amount of time available for the training session. Schedule the session and arrange for the facility and the audiovisual equipment (projector, screen, sound system, compter). Gather the other materials you will need.

- Determine food and beverage requirements and make the necessary arrangements.

- Invite participants. Send confirmation with an agenda or a list of the modules to be covered.

- Prepare copies of training materials to match your enrollment.

- Practice. Carefully review the training materials. Be prepared to respond to questions that the materials and activities are likely to generate. Review the PowerPoint presentation and practice in front of a friend or colleague so you're comfortable with the key points and slide transitions and have a solid understanding of the topic.

- Decide on the method you will use for splitting the class into working groups (for example, counting off or asking participants to choose their own partners, and so forth).

- For discussion questions, prepare answers to help the pairs share their answers (to prime the pump) and use real-life scenarios from your organization.

◆ As much as possible, check all arrangements in the training room the night before (when training starts in the morning) or two to three hours prior to the start of the session.

◆ Prepare the evaluation form (see Appendix B) for the attendees so that you can receive feedback and have information for improving the module for future training sessions.

◆ After the session, provide the evaluation results and any post-training assignments to the participants' managers. You also may wish to provide a summary report of any insights you obtained during the training.

◆ ◆ ◆

Now that your salespeople have honed their communication skills and understand the basic components of communication, it's time they learn to make that important presentation. Chapter 10 offers the secrets to delivering a memorable presentation.

Training Instrument 9–1
Worksheet: Communicating in Person

Preparation

1. What is the intention of the communication?

2. What is the essence of the message?

3. What offer/value will you deliver in the communication?

4. What is your request, if any?

Draft the Message

1. Personalized opening and closing:

2. Big picture to details:

3. Present your purpose (value/request, if any):

4. Recap key points and identify next step:

continued on next page

Training Instrument 9–1, continued
Worksheet: Communicating in Person

Check for Unintended Consequences

1. What are the possible consequences?

2. Are any of them negative to the task, relationship, or your organization?

Refine

1. Does the message reflect your organization's personality?

2. Have you used imagery where possible?

3. Are you in keeping with your organization's tone/manner?

4. Were you able to deliver any key messages?

5. Is the communication aligned with the client's style and in keeping with your style?

Training Instrument 9–2

Worksheet: Communicating by Telephone

Preparation

1. What is the intention of the communication?

2. What is the essence of the message?

3. What offer/value will you deliver in the communication?

4. What is your request, if any?

Draft the Message

1. Personalized opening and closing:

2. Big picture to details:

3. Present your purpose (value/request, if any):

4. Recap key points and identify next step:

continued on next page

Training Instrument 9–2, continued

Worksheet: Communicating by Telephone

Check for Unintended Consequences

1. What are the possible consequences?

2. Are any of them negative to the task, relationship, or your organization?

Refine

1. Does the message reflect your organization's personality?

2. Are you in keeping with your organization's tone/manner?

3. Were you able to deliver any key messages?

4. Is the communication aligned with the client's style and in keeping with your style?

Training Instrument 9–3

Worksheet: Communicating in Writing by Letter, Email, or Fax

Preparation

1. What is the intention of the communication?

2. What is the essence of the message?

3. What offer/value will you deliver in the communication?

4. What is your request, if any?

Draft the Message

1. Personalized opening and closing:

2. Big picture to details:

3. Present your purpose (value/request, if any):

4. Recap key points and identify next step:

continued on next page

Training Instrument 9–3, continued

Worksheet: Communicating in Writing by Letter, Email, or Fax

Check for Unintended Consequences

1. What are the possible consequences?

2. Are any of them negative to the task, relationship, or your organization?

Refine

1. Does the message reflect your organization's personality?

2. Have you used imagery where possible?

3. Are you in keeping with your organization's tone/manner?

4. Were you able to deliver any key messages?

5. Is the communication aligned with the client's style and in keeping with your style?

Tool 9–1

Worksheet Example: Communicating in Person

Preparation

1. What is the intention of the communication?

   Introduce our new product.

2. What is the essence of the message?

   Check and make sure our research is accurate about our new product relative to the client's situation.

3. What offer/value will you deliver in the communication?

   Offer detailed information from our research and compare it to the client's current situation.

4. What is your request, if any?

   To review the research during the sales call and determine if a product trial makes sense.

Draft the Message

1. Personalized opening and closing:

   Opening: *I am pleased to have this opportunity to show you our new product and to thank you for expressing such interest in the product during our phone call last week.*

   Closing: *based on a key point brought up in the meeting.*

2. Big picture to details:

   Big picture: *Research summary.*

   Middle: *How the product has been used within the client's industry.*

   Details: *Particular data that would affect the client specifically.*

3. Present your purpose (value/request, if any):

   Now that I have presented the data in the report, can we review your thoughts about how the product might apply to you? Do you see any direct applications and, if so, what are they? What concerns do you have at this point about the product? What further information might you need to schedule a product trial?

4. Recap key points and identify next step:

   These would be determined from the answers to my questions.

continued on next page

Tool 9–1, continued

Worksheet Example: Communicating in Person

Check for Unintended Consequences

1. What are the possible consequences?

   I might not be able to go over all the information in a 20-minute meeting.

   The client might feel rushed to make a decision and thus misinterpret my desire to ensure that the product makes sense for the client.

   The information might be boring so that when I get to the questions the client might not pay attention.

2. Are any of them negative to the task, relationship, or your organization?

   The first and third consequences would be negative to the task, and the second consequence probably would not help the relationship.

Refine

1. Does the message reflect your organization's personality? *Yes*

2. Have you used imagery where possible? *Yes, the actual report*

3. Are you in keeping with your organization's tone/manner? *Yes*

4. Were you able to deliver any key messages? *Not sure*

5. Is the communication aligned with the client's style and in keeping with your style? *Not with the client's style because there is too much data; yes as to my style because I like to show lots of proof.*

   Shorten the intro to say thanks for the time and to say that I hope the information I brought lives up to the interest the client expressed on the phone.

   Tell the client that I will show some relevant pieces of the research and then ask a few questions. Let the client know that I have the entire report with me in case of any detail-type questions.

   Make sure the client knows that I want to ensure that the product makes sense in the client's opinion before asking for a product trial.

   Share the data relevant to the client's situation and get right into the questions. Look for an opening to share a key message about the product that marketing has developed.

   Personal note: watch my body language so that the client notices that I am paying close attention to his questions and comments.

   At 15 minutes, ask permission to go over the 20 minutes if the client is asking questions or providing more information. I want to show respect for her time.

Tool 9–2

Worksheet Example: Communicating by Telephone

Preparation

1. What is the intention of the communication?

   Get an appointment to present new product line.

2. What is the essence of the message?

   I will not waste the client's time, and I believe our new products will be of benefit.

3. What offer/value will you deliver in the communication?

   Explain how the new product will save money.

4. What is your request, if any?

   Set an appointment (20–30 minutes).

Draft the Message

1. Personalized opening and closing:

   Opening: *Mr. or Ms. XXX, thank you for taking my call. The purpose of my call today is to give you a brief overview of our new product line and then, if the products are of interest, to set up an appointment to review the products in more detail. Do you have five minutes for this call?*

   Closing: *based on a key point brought up in the call.*

2. Big picture to details

   Big picture: *New products designed for the client's work environment.*

   Middle: *Products have completed trial runs.*

   Details: *Cost savings have ranged from 15 percent to 25 percent.*

3. Present your purpose (value/request, if any):

   I believe our new products can save you money. To explain in more detail about how the products work, I would like to have a 20- to 30-minute meeting with you. If you agree with my thinking, when would be a good day and time to meet?

4. Recap key points and identify next step:

   These would be determined from the answers to my questions.

continued on next page

Tool 9–2, continued

Worksheet Example: Communicating by Telephone

Check for Unintended Consequences

1. What are the possible consequences?

    Being too formal with this client might work against me.

    I might run out of time before I explain the new product's benefits.

    If I sound rushed the client might not believe me.

2. Are any of them negative to the task, relationship, or your organization?

    The first consequence would be negative to the task, and the other two consequences would adversely affect the task and the relationship.

Refine

1. Does the message reflect your organization's personality? *Yes*

2. Have you used imagery where possible? *Not applicable*

3. Are you in keeping with your organization's tone/manner? *Yes*

4. Were you able to deliver any key messages? *Yes*

5. Is the communication aligned with the client's style and in keeping with your style?
    Not to the client's style because this client is more informal; yes to my style because I like to get to the point.

    Be more informal with the intro and mention something from the last meeting/phone call to let the client know that I remember topics other than business.

    Tell the client that rather than trying to explain some of the basic benefits of the new product over the phone, a face-to-face meeting would be more effective.

    Focus more on the client and setting up the appointment as opposed to talking about the new product.

Tool 9–3
Worksheet: Communicating in Writing by Email

Preparation

1. What is the intention of the communication?

   To get a response to my previous email messages.

2. What is the essence of the message?

   I want to accommodate the client's wishes.

3. What offer/value will you deliver in the communication?

   Accommodate the client's wishes.

4. What is your request, if any?

   Answer my email messages.

Draft the Message

1. Personalized opening and closing:

   Opening: *Mr. or Ms. XXX, it is our desire to accommodate your wishes. We have responded X times to your request for information, and to date we have not received your reply.*

   Closing: *If you wish to receive further email communication from me, please respond to this message in the next 10 days. Otherwise, I will return your contact information to our corporate marketing department for periodic updates.*

2. Big picture to details:

   Not applicable in this situation

3. Present your purpose (value/request, if any):

   Perhaps your interest has changed, and if this is the case, we again would like to accommodate your wishes by discontinuing (or concluding) email correspondence.

4. Recap key points and identify next step:

   Not applicable in this situation

continued on next page

Tool 9–3, continued
Worksheet: Communicating in Writing by Email

Check for Unintended Consequences

1. What are the possible consequences?

   Client might ignore this email as well.

   Client might respond to this email.

   Email could be screened as spam.

2. Are any of them negative to the task, relationship, or your organization?

   The first and third consequences would be negative to the task and relationship.

Refine

1. Does the message reflect your organization's personality? *Yes*

2. Have you used imagery where possible? *Not applicable*

3. Are you in keeping with your organization's tone/manner? *Yes*

4. Were you able to deliver any key messages? *Yes*

5. Is the communication aligned with the client's style and in keeping with your style? *Client's style is not known so it is best to default to polite/formal language.*

   Subject line of the email will be important to make sure the message is not screened as spam. Use the date of the client's original request: Responding to your request for info on XX/XX/XX.

Slide 9–1

**Communicating—
A Basic Formula**

*"I didn't have time to write a short letter,
so I wrote a long one instead."*
– Mark Twain

Slide 9–2

Communicating

The Components

- 55% Body language
- 38% Tone
- 7% Words

Slide 9–3

Communicating

- Face-to-Face = 100%

- Telephone = 45%

- Written = 7%

Slide 9–4

Communicating

A Basic Formula

- Prepare
- Draft the message
- Check for unintended consequences
- Refine

Slide 9–5

Communicating

Preparation

- What is the intention of the communication?
- What is the essence of the message?
- What value will you deliver to the recipient?
- What is your request, if any?

Slide 9–6

Communicating

Draft the Message

- Write your personalized opening and closing.
- Always start with the big picture and follow with the details.
- Present your purpose:
  - your value
  - your request, if any.
- Recap the key points and identify the next step.

Slide 9–7

Communicating

Check for Unintended Consequences

- What are the possible consequences?
- Are any of them negative to the task, the relationship, or your organization?

Slide 9–8

Communicating

Refine

- Does the message reflect your organization's personality?
- Have you used imagery where possible?
- Were you able to deliver any key messages?
- Is the communication aligned with client's style and in keeping with your style?

Slide 9–9

Communicating

**Applying the Model to
In-Person Communications**

Slide 9–10

Communicating

- Select 1–2 customers whom you will see in person within the next 5–7 days.
- Use the Communicating in Person Worksheet to design your communication.
- After completing the first three steps of the worksheet, find a partner and together refine your communication.
- Report to the group what you have learned.

Slide 9–11

Communicating

**Applying the Model to
Telephone Communications**

Slide 9–12

Communicating

- Select 1–2 customers whom you will call within the next 5–7 days.
- Use the Communicating by Telephone Worksheet to design your communication.
- After completing the first three steps of the worksheet, find a partner and together refine your communication.
- Report to the group what you have learned.

Slide 9–13

Communicating

Applying the Model to
Written Communications

Slide 9–14

Communicating

- Select a customer to whom you will send an important email message within the next 5–7 days.
- Use the Communicating in Writing Worksheet to design your communication.
- After completing the first three steps of the worksheet, find a partner and together refine your communication.
- Report to the group what you have learned.

Slide 9–15

Recap

- What have you learned from this module?
- What will you use right away in your work? Why?
- How will you use what you have learned?
- What is an effective way for you to actively improve your communicating skills? Why?
- How will you know your actions are producing results?

Slide 9–16

**Communicating—
A Basic Formula**

End of the Module

Communicating: Presentations Module

What's in This Chapter?

- A sales module that teaches sales personnel how to create memorable presentations

- A method that shows how to engage all five senses of your audience

- Tips and techniques that teach how to personalize each presentation

Sometimes a salesperson has only one chance at a presentation to get the business. This module is designed to help with important presentations. Some of these important presentations are at trade shows, in formal written proposal, and in verbal presentations to a group. In each of these situations, the customer often compares several presentations as part of the decision-making process.

It is common sense then to make the presentation memorable. This entails going beyond showing how a product or service is right for the customer and differentiating the presentation from the competitor's presentation. To accomplish this the presentation needs to engage the customer's senses (people acquire information differently—some are visual, others rely more on their hearing or the sense of touch [kinesthetic]), be customized, enhance the relationship, and be dynamic. The presentation must be professional, straightforward, and positive.

Training Objective

The purpose of this module is to provide insights into effective presentations and ideas that fully engage the customer.

Key Points in This Module

- Preparation and creative thinking help make presentations that get business.

- Engage the customer's senses to assist getting your key points across.

- A dynamic presentation can create a memorable impression.

- Presentations can enhance relationships, which creates customer loyalty.

- Customers in today's marketplace expect customized presentations.

- Creativity is good, but the basics—proper grammar, positive language, and honesty—are just as important.

Materials

- Two flipchart easels with paper and colored markers

- LCD projector, screen, and computer for running the PowerPoint presentation

- Paper for the participants to use in taking notes

- Training Instrument 10–1: Presentation Worksheet

- Tool 10–1: Worksheet Example: Presentation

- PowerPoint slides 10–1 through 10–12. Copies of the slides for this module, *Presentations.ppt,* are included at the end of this chapter.

- Extra flipchart paper and markers for the structured exercises

- Brochures and other marketing collateral pieces for the structured exercises

- Examples of presentations that your organization currently uses (written, PowerPoint, and so forth)

- *Optional:* fun materials for the structured exercises, such as magazine picture clippings, glitter, balloons, poster boards, paper glue, and anything else your imagination comes up with

CD Resources

Materials for this module appear both in this workbook and as electronic files on the CD that accompanies the book. To access the files, insert the CD and look at its "PDF Files" directory for the training instruments and tools needed. The PowerPoint presentation is also on the CD. You will find more detailed instructions and help in locating files on the CD by referring to Appendix C, "Using the Compact Disc," at the back of the workbook.

Sample Agenda

9:00 a.m.   Show slide 10–1. Here is another Mark Twain quote that can be interpreted to mean that all impromptu speeches are based in some type of preparation. The same can be said about the presentations salespeople make to customers, especially those that the customer will use for a decision. This module has a formula for developing effective presentations that will engage customers at various levels.

9:05   Show slide 10–2. Ask the participants about the different types of presentations that sales professionals make. List their answers on a flipchart. After you list all the different types of presentations, ask the group which ones pertain to the customer making an important decision. Some possible responses are

   ◆   written (proposal, letter of introduction, introductory email)

   ◆   oral (telephone, in person, to a committee)

   ◆   group

   ◆   PowerPoint

   ◆   trade show.

   Tell the group that this module focuses on proposals, group presentations, and trade shows.

9:10   Show slide 10–3. (**Note to facilitator:** This is a transition slide allowing you to read the key points and say that you will go through each point in detail.)

Table 10–1

Slide Information for the Presentations Module

NUMBER	TITLE/TOPIC	DESCRIPTION	TIME
10–1	Title slide: Presentations	Lets the class get settled and lets the facilitator welcome the group as appropriate	2 minutes
10–2	What are the different types of presentations?	Discussion question	2–3 minutes
10–3	Components of effective presentations	Six components	1 minute
10–4	Five-sensing and prepared components	Key points	2–3 minutes
10–5	Professional component	Key points	1 minute
10–6	Positive-language component	Key points and discussion question	2–3 minutes
10–7	Relationship-focused component	Key points	2–3 minutes
10–8	Dynamic component	Definition	10 seconds
10–9	Dynamic component	Key points	2–3 minutes
10–10	Practice	Structured exercise	30–45 minutes
10–11	Recap	Structured exercise	10–15 minutes
10–12	End of the module		

9:15 Show slide 10–4. Tell the participants that "five-sensing" means engaging as many of a customer's senses as possible during the presentation. Note that salespeople should be creative in finding ways to engage the customer's senses of sight, hearing, touch, smell, and taste. For example, in a written proposal, use pictures to make key points. If PowerPoint presentations are used, add music or sounds. Let the customer touch the product or something that represents the service.

The purpose of engaging the senses is linked to how people prefer to learn or receive information. Some people are visual (they say things like, "I see what you mean"); some depend on listening (they say things like, "I hear you"); and others are kinesthetic (that is, they need movement) or use touch (they might want to hold something while they talk).

If the salesperson knows the customer's dominant sense, he or she can build the presentation around this knowledge. If she or he doesn't know, then building a presentation to engage all the senses provides the opportunity for getting key points across effectively.

Another important point: Most human beings remember more when they are physically engaged. Think about a television cooking show—it has movement and sound and the chef describes how the food has a wonderful aroma and taste.

Obtain some presentation examples from your organization so that your salespeople can understand the applicability to their work. For example, a ski resort sent their proposal via overnight shipment with a chest of snow and fresh pine boughs. The proposal started off with instructions for making a small snowman. The proposal engaged sight (written proposal, snow, and boughs), touch (shaping the snowman), sound (sound of packing the snow into shapes), and smell (pine boughs).

Ask participants how they can engage the senses of their customers in presentations. (Use the types of presentations identified in the first discussion question.)

PREPARED PRESENTATIONS

A prepared presentation is planned, and not canned—customized rather than standardized. And it is tuned to the customer's style. If the customer uses more data than intuition to make decisions, then the presentation should use numbers and spreadsheets. If the customer focuses on the big picture, the presentation should use summaries and key points with details as an addendum.

9:25   Show slide 10–5. Tell the participants that the first requirement of a professional presentation is to be clear about its purpose. Sometimes presentations miss this important point, and the customer is left to interpret the purpose. This is just like not asking for the business.

Examples of purpose statements include

◆   *The purpose of this presentation is to provide you with the information necessary to make the decision best suited for your business.*

◆   *We want to prove to you that our product will support your forecasted growth for the next three years.*

◆   *This proposal has been designed to show how our service meets and exceeds your specifications.*

◆   *This presentation is about showing you why we want your business and how we will earn it.*

The other aspects of a professional presentation include proper grammar, correct spelling, consistent font and font size, easy-to-read formatting, limited use of jargon, and the like. In oral presentations, make sure the equipment works and that the presenter knows the script.

9:30   Show slide 10–6. Tell the participants that any presentation should talk to the customer in the second person.

Here's an example of speaking in the second person: "When using the XYZ product, *you* will find that all of your standards have been met." The alternative comment does not add that personal touch: "We think our product will meet the standards."

The purpose of using the second person is to focus on and talk directly to the customer and to provide an opportunity for the customer to think directly about using this product or service.

As much as possible, avoid negative words when making presentations because they can create an effect that's opposite to what was intended.

Here is a non-sales example: It's a warm summer day and children are playing in the yard. One after another they run into the house and slam the door. The mother yells at them, "Don't slam that door!"

Ask participants what mental picture they see? What picture would they see if the mother said, "Next time, please shut the door gently"?

Another way to use positive language is to let the customer know what you *can* do instead of what you can't do. Ask participants to change the following statements into positive language:

♦ We can't lower the price. (Possible change: Our price is based on the specifications provided.)

♦ We can't do that. (Possible change: Thank you for bringing that point up because it's one of the limitations of our product.)

♦ We cannot do that. (Possible change: That is one activity that our service is unable to do.)

Ask the group for other often-used negative statements and ask participants to rephrase them positively.

9:35   Show slide 10–7. Tell participants that excellent presentations subtly let the customer know that the salesperson values the relationship and that the customer provides more than just potential revenue.

Some simple ways to be relationship focused are to use the customer's name in the presentation and repeat important comments that the customer has made. For example, if the customer said that her company had recently set a new strategy and she was excited about it, mention it in the presentation.

The salesperson should ask himself or herself if this presentation will enhance the relationship and make the customer feel special. Also, the presentation should be tuned to the customer's natural style for receiving information and interaction.

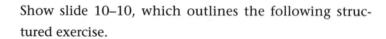

9:40   Show slide 10–8. Note the slide contents and move to the next slide.

9:42   Show slide 10–9. Tell the participants that it is important to use different colors in a presentation (whether presented on an easel or as a PowerPoint slide). Show movement to keep the customer interested in the presentation. For written or PowerPoint presentations, use bold, italics, and underlines.

Graphics are especially useful in presentations. The pictures engage the creative part of the customer's brain, and the words describing the picture involve the logical part of the brain. Being dynamic makes the presentation memorable and helps it stand out from the competition.

9:45   Show slide 10–10, which outlines the following structured exercise.

Structured Exercise 10–1

Step 1: Split the class into pairs or small groups of three or four people

Step 2: Have each group select one of the presentation types identified at the beginning of the module.

Step 3: Ask each group to develop a presentation using the components of a presentation discussed in this module. Distribute copies of Training Instrument 10–1 and Tool 10–1. Also provide flipchart paper, letterhead, company logos, colored markers, product brochures, and other marketing materials for the class to use. Encourage lots of creativity!

After 30–45 minutes, have each group practice its presentation in front of the class.

10:15 Show slide 10–11. The following exercise will help the participants capture their learning and prepare to use their new knowledge on the job.

Structured Exercise 10–2

Step 1: Put the class into pairs and ask each pair to answer the questions on the slide. After 5–10 minutes have each pair share its answers.

Step 2: *Optional:* Ask the participants to write out their answers so they can be given to their managers for follow-up after the training.

10:30 Show slide 10–12. Finish this module by commenting on the creativity of the participants and say that you look forward to even more creativity with future presentations.

What to Do Next

◆ Review Table 1–1: Sales Training Modules Matrix for help in determining how best to use the module in this chapter and the type of sales personnel who would benefit. Also review the matrix and the sales gap analyses completed by the sales personnel to determine which other modules you might want to use. Finally, review the information in chapter 1 on how best to use this book to fit your situation.

◆ For the first few modules you facilitate, plan on one hour of preparation for every hour of facilitation. As you gain experience with the modules, plan on 20 minutes of preparation for every hour of facilitation.

◆ Determine how much time is available for the training session. Schedule the session and arrange for the facility and the audiovisual equipment (projector, sound system, computer). Gather whatever other materials you will need.

◆ Determine food and beverage requirements and make necessary arrangements.

◆ Invite participants and send confirmation with an agenda or a list of the modules to be covered.

◆ Prepare copies of training materials to match your enrollment.

◆   Practice. Carefully review the training materials. Be prepared to respond to questions that the materials and activities are likely to generate. Review the PowerPoint presentation and practice in front of a friend or colleague so you're comfortable with the key points and slide transitions and have a solid understanding of the topic.

◆   Based on the number of participants, determine how you will conduct the structured exercises (pairs, trios, or small groups) and the method you will use for splitting the class into working groups (for example, counting off or asking participants to select their own partners, and so forth).

◆   As much as possible, check all arrangements in the training room the night before (when training starts in the morning) or two to three hours prior to the start of the session.

◆   Prepare the evaluation form (see Appendix B) for the attendees so that you can receive feedback and have information for improving the module for future training sessions.

◆   After the session, provide the evaluation results and any post-training assignments to the participants' managers. You also may wish to provide a summary report of any insights you obtained during the training.

◆ ◆ ◆

When delivering presentations—whether via the phone or in person—certain trigger words will create a lasting impression on customers. Two of those words are "features" and "benefits." Your salespeople need to learn the importance of features and benefits, and the essential difference between the two. All of that is covered in the next chapter.

Training Instrument 10–1
Presentation Worksheet

Client: _____

Type of presentation: _____

Purpose of presentation: _____

Five-sensing—Which, why, and how?

How can I enhance the relationship with this presentation?

How can I animate this presentation?

Double-check:

1. Is the presentation customized?

2. Is it professional?

3. Is it honest/straightforward?

4. Is positive language used?

Tool 10–1
Worksheet Example: Presentation

Client: *RAMI Design Group*

Type of presentation: *Oral to the steering committee*

Purpose of presentation: *Get into finals*

Five-sensing—Which, why, and how?

Sight—get their attention and show them that we can produce stunning graphics; when the graphics are presented, darken the room and have spotlights on the graphics.

Sound—use music to anchor their memory even more about our presentation.

Touch—engage the committee physically by having them touch some of the graphics that are embossed; put the graphics into a box with a shroud so the members have to feel the graphic before seeing it.

How can I enhance the relationship with this presentation?

Personalize each presentation packet that we leave behind. Review the bios of each committee member and select a graphic that would appeal to each member; present the graphic as a gift.

How can I animate this presentation?

As the committee enters the room, have a DVD playing the scenes from Cool Hand Luke *(the part about the failure to communicate).*

Employ prepared flipcharts using multicolored markers instead of PowerPoint graphics.

After each graphic is shown, put it on a large banner that we are using to keep track of the meetings proceedings; the banner then becomes the meeting minutes for the client to keep.

Double-check:

1. Is the presentation customized?

2. Is it professional?

3. Is it honest/straightforward?

4. Is positive language used?

Slide 10–1

Presentations

"It usually takes more than three weeks to prepare a good impromptu speech."
– Mark Twain

Slide 10–2

Presentations

What are the different types
of presentations that
we make?

Slide 10–3

Presentations

**Characteristics of Effective
Presentations**

- Five–sensing
- Prepared
- Professional
- Uses positive language
- Relationship focused
- Dynamic

Slide 10–4

Presentations

- *Five–sensing*
  - Sight
  - Sound
  - Smell
  - Touch
  - Taste
- *Prepared*
  - Planned, not canned
  - Customized
  - Tuned to the customer's style

Slide 10–5

Presentations

- *Professional*
  - Purpose of the presentation is clear.
  - Proper grammar, correct spelling, and clear formatting are used.

Slide 10–6

Presentations

- *Uses positive language*
  - Use the second–person approach.
  - Avoid using the word "not."
  - Tell the customer what <u>can</u> be done vs. what <u>can't</u> be done.

Slide 10–7

Presentations

- *Relationship focused*
  - Enhance the relationship.
  - Use the customer's name.
  - Use comments the customer has made.
  - Again, tune to the customer's style.

Slide 10–8

Presentations

Dynamic
Energetic – Forceful – Productive

Slide 10–9

Presentations

- Use colors
- Show——>*movement*
- **BOLD** – *Italics* – <u>Underline</u>
- Use graphics

Slide 10–10

Practice

- In pairs or groups, select a type of presentation (trade show, PowerPoint, proposal, or oral).
- Using the presentation components, develop a presentation.
- Practice the presentation in front of your colleagues.

Slide 10–11

Recap

- What have you learned from this module?
- What will you use right away in your work? Why?
- How will you use what you have learned?
- What is an effective way for you to actively improve your communicating skills? Why?
- How will you know your actions are producing results?

Slide 10–12

Presentations

End of the Module

◆

Communicating: Features, Benefits, and Proof Module

What's in This Chapter?

- ◆ Discussion of the important difference between features and benefits

- ◆ A sales module that teaches how to develop personalized and powerful benefit statements for each client

- ◆ Exercises that participants can put into practice immediately with their present clients

We've all heard the classic feature/benefit sales and marketing stuff before. Beyond learning the distinction between features and benefits, the real value is in the customization of benefit statements for each customer. Salespeople need to think for a moment about who their customers are. Customers represent buying power and are therefore constantly bombarded by mass-marketing messages from every conceivable source. But because there is no such creature as an *average* customer, customers probably ignore basic, expected, or even slick types of marketing or sales talk.

If a salesperson is just a "talking brochure," customers might as well visit the Web site or read the collateral materials on their own. Bringing the benefits to life in a way that appeals personally to each customer is one more way to earn the customer's trust and facilitate his or her decision-making process.

The key to developing powerful, customized benefit statements is to understand the customer's conditions of satisfaction, particularly the implicit ones. When salespeople become fluent with a repertoire of benefit statements they can easily customize on the spot.

This module works best if attendees have similar ranges of experience. Inexperienced salespeople attending this module will need to have basic product knowledge. For inexperienced salespeople you will need some examples of benefit statements that your sales team already is using to help the participants develop their own.

Experienced salespeople likely work at a faster pace and on rather more advanced benefit statements. When working with an experienced group, offer this module as a chance to focus on sharpening their skills by letting them develop and practice new, more advanced benefit statements.

Be careful about using statements from the marketing or public relations departments because these statements may read well in a brochure but often are less effective in a sales environment.

Training Objective

This module provides a simple method for creating and using benefit statements.

Key Points in This Module

- This module is less about learning a new skill than it is about sharpening an existing skill.

- No matter how many times a salesperson has gone through features-and-benefits training, she or he can still improve benefit statements.

- Customized benefit statements are very powerful because they are linked to the customer's specific conditions of satisfaction.

- Salespeople should develop statements in their own language and style so they are comfortable and believable when they speak.

Materials

- Two flipchart easels with paper and colored markers

- LCD projector, screen, and computer for running the PowerPoint presentation

- Paper for the participants to use in taking notes

- Training Instrument 11–1: Features, Benefits, and Proof Worksheet

- Tool 11–1: Worksheet Example: Features, Benefits, and Proof

- ◆ PowerPoint slides 11–1 through 11–8. Copies of the slides for this module, *Features and Benefits.ppt,* are included at the end of this chapter.

- ◆ *Optional:* a pad of 3 x 5-inch notepaper for each participant

- ◆ *Optional:* one Sharpie-style marker for each participant

CD Resources

Materials for this module appear both in this workbook and as electronic files on the CD that accompanies the book. To access the files, insert the CD and look at its "PDF Files" directory for the training instruments and tools needed. The PowerPoint presentation is also on the CD. You will find more detailed instructions and help in locating files on the CD by referring to Appendix C, "Using the Compact Disc," at the back of the workbook.

Sample Agenda

9:00 a.m.   Show slide 11–1. Ask the participants the question on the slide: "What does it mean to be a talking brochure?" Here are some potential answers from the participants:

- ◆ Salesperson would sound insincere or fake to the customer.

- ◆ Customers could question the salesperson's competency if they've already read about the product or service on the Web site or in a brochure.

- ◆ The customer might feel like he's being treated like just a number rather than as an individual.

- ◆ The customer might think she's dealing with just another typical salesperson and go straight to price.

- ◆ The customer could think talking with this type of salesperson is a waste of time.

9:05   Show slide 11–2. Say that there are many approaches to developing benefit statements. In this module participants will begin by identifying the two parts of a feature:

Table 11–1

Slide Information for the Features, Benefits, and Proof Module

NUMBER	TITLE/TOPIC	DESCRIPTION	TIME
11–1	Title slide: Features, benefits, and proof	Enables the class to get settled and the facilitator to welcome the group as appropriate	2–5 minutes
11–2	Two parts of a feature	Name and purpose	1 minute
11–3	What turns a feature into a benefit	Two reasons	1 minute
11–4	Types of proof	Five examples	1 minute
11–5	What types of proof are available to you?	Discussion question	2–3 minutes
11–6	Practice	Structured exercise	15–20 minutes
11–7	Recap	Structured exercise	10–15 minutes
11–8	End of the module		

1. **A feature is a fact about a product or service, as distinguished from an opinion.** Here's an example: "We offer 24-hour customer service" vs. "We offer great customer service." (**Note to facilitator:** Use some of the features from your organization's products or services as examples. Use specific language and avoid brochure talk.)

2. **A feature has a purpose for the customer.** The purposes of features are typically for convenience, saving money, adding value, increasing revenue opportunities, and so forth.

Structured Exercise 11–1

Step 1: Split the group into pairs.

Step 2: Have the pairs identify purposes of the key features of their products or services. Allow 5–10 minutes.

Step 3: Ask each pair to share its work with the group.

Step 4: Write the responses on a flipchart.

This activity could lead to an interesting discussion among the participants based on the different perceptions they have of purposes for the same features.

9:15

Show slide 11–3. Tell the participants that features become benefits when they address a customer's conditions of satisfaction and can provide a positive response to the question, "So what?" To accomplish this, the benefit statements your salespeople create must clearly communicate how features satisfy a specific priority or address a customer's concerns.

Note to facilitator: As much as possible, provide examples of benefit statements for the class. You can use the examples from Tool 11–1 as a starter. When highlighting examples be sure to share the condition of satisfaction, concern, or priority that the benefit statement addresses.

9:25

Show slide 11–4. Say that many customers are skeptical of what a salesperson says or may be curious about the background or history of information presented. To address either skepticism or simple curiosity, proof and support are helpful tools. Different types of support include

♦ fact sheets or specification sheets

♦ brochures and other marketing materials (news releases, Web site, and the like)

♦ FAQs (frequently asked questions)

♦ letters from customers

♦ third-party endorsements (articles, surveys, and so forth).

9:30

Show slide 11–5. Use the question on the slide to prompt answers about what types of support are available. This is a brainstorming session to generate ideas about all possible types and examples of support available or easily created.

You can either write the ideas on a flipchart or provide 3 x 5-inch notepads and have each participant write one idea per note. The purpose of the discussion is to identify as many examples as possible and to discover some examples that the participants may not have thought of before.

9:35 Show slide 11–6, which outlines the following structured exercise.

Structured Exercise 11–2

Step 1: Have each participant select two or three customers to whom they will make sales presentations in the next week.

Step 2: Have participants create one or two benefit statements for each customer using Training Instrument 11–1 and Tool 11–1. Allow 10–15 minutes. Participants should each produce two to six statements using different features intended for specific customers.

Step 3: Have them identify specific items of proof or support for each presentation they will make.

Step 4: Split the group into pairs so they can practice using their benefit statements out loud. They should practice each benefit statement at least once.

Step 5: For each benefit statement the listening partner should ask what concerns or conditions of satisfaction cause the feature to become a benefit and how the benefit statement answers the "so what?" question.

9:50 Show slide 11–7. Tell the participants the following exercise will help them capture their learning and prepare to use their new knowledge on the job.

Structured Exercise 11–3

Step 1: Split the class into pairs.

Step 2: Ask each pair to answer the questions on the slide. Allow 5–10 minutes.

Step 3: Have each pair share its answers with the group. *Option:* Ask the participants to write their answers so they can be given to their managers for follow-up after the training.

10:00   Show slide 11–8. Thank the participants for their work and ask them to share any benefit statements they create in the future so that everyone can learn from them.

What to Do Next

◆ Review Table 1–1: Sales Training Modules Matrix for help in determining how best to use the module in this chapter and the type of sales personnel who would benefit. Also review the matrix and the sales gap analyses completed by the sales personnel to determine which other modules you might want to use. Finally, review the information in chapter 1 on how best to use this book to fit your situation.

◆ For the first few modules you facilitate, plan on one hour of preparation for every hour of facilitation. As you gain experience with the modules, plan on 20 minutes of preparation for every hour of facilitation.

◆ Determine how much time is available for the training session. Schedule the session and arrange for the facility and the audiovisual equipment (projector, screen, sound system, computer). Gather the other materials you will need.

◆ Determine food and beverage requirements and make necessary arrangements.

◆ Invite participants and send confirmation with an agenda or a list of the modules to be covered.

◆ Prepare copies of training materials to match your enrollment.

◆ Practice. Carefully review the training materials. Be prepared to respond to questions that the materials and activities are likely to generate. Review the PowerPoint presentation and practice in front of a friend or colleague so you grow comfortable with the key points and slide transitions and have a solid understanding of the topic.

◆ Choose the method you will use for splitting the class into working groups (for example, counting off or asking each participant to choose a partner, and so forth).

◆ As much as possible, check all arrangements in the training room the night before (when training starts in the morning) or two to three hours prior to the start of the session.

◆ Prepare the evaluation form (see Appendix B) for the attendees so that you can receive feedback and have information for improving the module for future training sessions.

◆ After the session, provide the evaluation results and any post-training assignments to the participants' managers. You also may wish to provide a summary report of any insights you obtained during the training.

◆ ◆ ◆

Your salespeople have mastered the art of relationship building, communication, and presentation. Now it's time to create a compelling offer. The next chapter offers a module you can use to train them to collaborate with clients and make offers that clients can't refuse.

Training Instrument 11–1
Features, Benefits, and Proof Worksheet

Feature and purpose

Benefit: Answers the question, "So what?"

Proof

Feature and purpose

Benefit: Answers the question, "So what?"

Proof

Tool 11–1
Worksheet Example: Features, Benefits, and Proof

Feature and Purpose

Feature: 24/7 Service/support via a toll-free number

Purpose: Support customers via telephone 24/7

Benefit: Answers the question, "So what?"

When your employees are working after the information technology (IT) department is closed, they can get support. (This is tied to condition of satisfaction about making sure employees can get support when IT is closed.)

Proof

Service/support fact sheets

Complimentary letters

JD Power survey

Feature and Purpose

Feature: High-speed eight-person ski lift

Purpose: Skiers spend less time in line and take more runs on the mountain

Benefit: Answers the question, "So what?"

You will have at least 15 percent more ski runs in a six-hour period for only 10 percent more in price than XYZ mountain has. (This is tied to condition of satisfaction about number of runs and competitor's pricing.)

Proof

Recent article in Ski magazine

Ski lift specifications

Brochure

Slide 11–1

Features, Benefits, and Proof

What does it mean to be a talking brochure?

Slide 11–2

Features, Benefits, and Proof

Two Parts to a Feature

1. Name or a basic description
2. The purpose of the feature

Slide 11–3

Features, Benefits, and Proof

What turns a feature into a benefit?

- It is linked to a customer's condition of satisfaction, concerns, or priorities.
- It answers the important question, "So what?"

Slide 11–4

Features, Benefits, and Proof

- Types of Proof:
  - Brochures and other marketing collateral
  - Fact sheets
  - FAQs [frequently asked questions]
  - Letters from customers
  - Third–party endorsements (articles and surveys)

Slide 11–5

Features, Benefits, and Proof

W0hat types of proof are available to you?

Slide 11–6

Practice

- Select 2–3 customers to whom you will present benefits in the next week.
- Write out 1–2 benefit statements per customer, using the Features, Benefits, and Proof Worksheet.
- With a partner, practice your benefit statements and proof orally.
- Each partner is to practice each benefit statement and proof at least once.
- The partner listening to the benefit statements asks what conditions of satisfaction or concerns turn the feature into a benefit.

Slide 11–7

Recap

- What have you learned from this module?
- What will you use right away in your work? Why?
- How will you use what you have learned?
- What is an effective way for you to actively improve your benefit statements? Why?
- How will you know your actions are producing results?

Slide 11–8

Features, Benefits, and Proof

End of the Module

Communicating: Compelling Offers Module

- A sales module that teaches how to create a compelling offer

- Instructions on how to collaborate with clients and eliminate the old-school style of manipulation

- An explanation of the difference between alignment and agreement and how that influences the decision-making process

The customer's conditions of satisfaction have been uncovered, the salesperson thinks that he or she knows the customer's style, and the two have aligned themselves. Now, it is time to make the offer, or in old sales terminology, go for the close. The phrase, "go for the close" often reminds people of the stereotypical manipulative sales processes. Myriad closing techniques have surfaced throughout the years: the puppy-dog close, the trial close, the take-away close, the limited-time-offer close. These methods intended first to get the sale and second to satisfy the customer. Today's customers know about these methods and prefer salespeople who want to collaborate with them, not manipulate them. Customers seek satisfaction with the products and services they buy *and* with their sales-process experience.

Using the advocacy model presented in this module, a salesperson can work collaboratively with customers to create compelling offers. By using the advocacy model, the salesperson shares her or his thinking process, in addition to the products of that thinking. The model creates shared understanding and direction and can turn words and ideas into a purchase decision. Conversely, the model can reveal missing key points or opinions that the customer has not articulated and so allows for further inquiry.

There are two prerequisite modules to this session: Conditions of Satisfaction (chapter 6) and Sales Mind Focus (chapter 4). Other modules that would be helpful include the Tasks and Relationships (chapter 5) and the previous Communicating modules (chapters 9–11).

Training Objective

This module provides a collaborative method that enables the salesperson and the customer to reach an agreement.

Key Points in This Module

◆ Today's customers want collaboration, not old-style manipulation.

◆ Compelling offers include the customer's conditions of satisfaction.

◆ A salesperson needs to align with the customer, which includes proper timing, before making a compelling offer.

◆ The advocacy model helps the salesperson share his or her thinking process as well as the product.

Materials

◆ Two flipchart easels with paper and colored markers

◆ LCD projector, screen, and computer for running the PowerPoint presentation

◆ Paper for the participants to use in taking notes

◆ PowerPoint slides 12–1 through 12–14. Copies of the slides for this module, *Compelling Offers.ppt,* are included at the end of this chapter.

CD Resources

Materials for this module appear both in this workbook and as electronic files on the CD that accompanies the book. To access the files, insert the CD and look at its "PDF Files" directory for the training instruments and tools needed. The PowerPoint presentation is also on the CD. You will find more detailed instructions and help in locating files on the CD by referring to Appendix C, "Using the Compact Disc," at the back of the workbook.

Sample Agenda

9:00 a.m. Show slide 12–1. Ask the participants this question: "How many of you remember the first *Godfather* movie, when Don Corleone was asked how he was able to convince a person to accept an offer? His answer was quite simple, 'I made him an offer he couldn't refuse.'" In this module we will learn a method for creating compelling offers that are hard to refuse. Unlike the Godfather's method, the advocacy model enables us to make our offers collaboratively with our customers.

Table 12–1

Slide Information for the Compelling Offers Module

NUMBER	TITLE/TOPIC	DESCRIPTION	TIME
12–1	Title slide: Compelling offers	Enables the class to get settled and the facilitator to welcome the group as appropriate	2 minutes 2 minutes
12–2	Components	Four components	1 minute
12–3	A collaborative approach	Shared understanding	1 minute
12–4	Advocacy model	Five parts of the model	1 minute
12–5	Example of advocacy	Example	1 minute
12–6	Example of advocacy, continued	Example	2 minutes
12–7	Example of advocacy	Example	1 minute
12–8	Example of advocacy, continued	Example and discussion questions	2–3 minutes
12–9	Unproductive advocacy	Example	1 minute
12–10	Productive advocacy	Components	1 minute
12–11	When would you use the advocacy model?	Discussion question	1–2 minutes
12–12	Practice	Structured exercise	20–25 minutes
12–13	Recap	Structured exercise	10–15 minutes
12–14	End of the module		

9:05   Show slide 12–2, which outlines the following components of a compelling offer:

- conditions of satisfaction

- alignment and timing

- appropriate language/style

- collaborative approach.

The conditions of satisfaction were covered in chapter 6. If a reminder is needed, ask the group about the implicit and explicit conditions of satisfaction they identified in that training session.

Customer alignment has been covered in various modules, including those dealing with tasks and relationships (chapter 5) and with different modes of communicating (chapters 9–11). Each customer has his or her own style for making decisions and reviewing information, and salespeople know it is important to align with the customer from those perspectives. When making compelling offers there are two additional aspects of alignment that must be addressed: the distinction between alignment and agreement and the timing of the offer.

Sometimes we confuse alignment with agreement. Ask the group, "How many of you have been in a situation where the customer said she liked the product or service and then didn't buy?" That's an example of confusing alignment with agreement. The customer is in alignment that the product or service is right for her, but for some reason she isn't ready to make an agreement.

This leads into the second aspect, timing. For a customer to accept an offer, he or she needs to be ready. If an offer is made too soon the customer might feel pressured, and if the offer is made too late the customer may have lost interest.

Taking a collaborative approach helps a salesperson test whether the offer is compelling and the timing is right without damaging the relationship or the sale.

9:10   Show slide 12–3. Tell the participants that the advocacy method creates a shared understanding and turns words and ideas into coordinated action. In sales, advocacy is used to make compelling offers, or it can work as part of the negotiation process. Advocacy lays forth a salesperson's thinking to the customer and allows the customer to examine that thinking.

9:15   Show slide 12–4. (**Note to facilitator:** This slide is intended to help you explain the components of advocacy before showing the examples on the following slides.)

1. **Own the offer.** This means that the salesperson makes it clear that he or she believes in the offer. The salesperson makes a declaration such as, "I believe this is the right product at the right price," rather than, "We think this product might work for you." The second statement can create an unintended interpretation by the customer that the salesperson is unsure or does not believe that the product is right.

2. **Present your thinking/reasons.** After making the declaration, the salesperson presents reasons that support the statement, including the customer's conditions of satisfaction, facts and data, and statements the customer has made.

3. **Check for understanding.** After sharing his or her reasons, the salesperson checks for understanding or agreement. If the customer says he doesn't understand or doesn't agree, the salesperson suspends the advocacy model and goes into inquiry mode to uncover concerns or other implicit conditions of satisfaction. The relationship still is intact at this point, and only the task of making the sale has slowed down.

4. **Derive deduction.** If the customer agrees or understands, then the salesperson explores the implications or results of the proposal. For example, the customer would save time or money or would outperform a competitor using the salesperson's product or service. These implications are important because they indi-

cate that the salesperson is tuned in to the customer's situation and thus create the benefits for purchasing the product or service.

5. **Invite responses.** After you share the implications, ask the customer for feedback on the offer. This brings the customer into the offer and invites her participation in making a compelling offer.

It is important that participants understand the collaborative approach that the advocacy model provides. They also need to know that it is equally vital to integrate their own natural or typical language into the model so that their behavior and embodiment of the model seems natural to the customer.

Let's turn now to some examples. (**Note to facilitator:** Slides 12–5 to 12–8 are examples of advocacy, and they set up discussion questions. The purpose of the questions is to prompt thinking and to generate ideas about how to begin customizing the language used in the model to each salesperson's style while aligning with the customer's style. Give the participants a few minutes to read each example and then ask the discussion questions. You may need to prompt participants for answers by giving examples such as the ones below.)

9:20   Show slides 12–5 to 12–8. There are two examples of advocacy here, each covering two slides. Give the group enough time to read the slides on their own.

When everyone has read the examples, discuss the following questions with the participants.

◆ **Own the offer.** What declarative statements would you use when making the offer? (*Examples:* I believe this is the right product for you. When you use our service, you will be saving money.)

◆ **Present reasons.** What are some different ways to present your reasons or your thinking? (*Examples:* Let me share my thinking. My thoughts behind why this is right for you are. . . .) (**Note to facilitator:** You want participants to create phrases that suit their personal styles, and some might feel that the phrase "my reasons for stating this are" is too formal.)

◆ **Check for understanding/alignment.** What phrase could you use other than this: "Does my thinking make sense to you?" (*Examples:* Is my thinking logical to you? Am I in alignment with your thinking?)

◆ **Derive deductions.** Do implications (which is another word for deductions here) have to be positive? (The answer is yes, or the customer might think he is being manipulated.) After reviewing the deductions section of the examples with the group, ask if the examples make sense. Ask if people can see a link between the declaration (reasons) and any conditions of satisfaction. If they don't see a link, ask if anyone in the group can come up with a real-life example using your organization's services or products.

◆ **Invite responses.** What other questions could you use to elicit the customer's feedback on your offer? (*Examples:* What is your initial thinking about our offer? Which parts of our offer make the most sense to you, and why?)

9:30   Show slide 12–9. Tell the participants that the purpose of this slide is to show how manipulative language takes the collaborative approach out of the advocacy model and makes it manipulative. Unproductive advocacy, at best, produces obstacles to a salesperson's understanding of the customer's position. At its worst, unproductive advocacy can lead a customer to think she is being manipulated.

9:45   Show slide 12–10. Tell the participants that productive advocacy exposes their reasoning, data, and concerns. Articulating one's thinking with the customer will help the customer understand why the salesperson is making a particular offer.

Salespeople should use facts wherever possible and announce any opinions or assumptions. Because facts are true or false, they are generally accepted (unless they are irrelevant to the discussion). Opinions and assumptions can be detrimental to coordinating action or group thinking unless they are announced and allowed to be explored. When sharing opinions or assumptions, the salesperson should explain the reasoning behind them and ask if they make sense to the customer. This lets the customer know that her input is wanted and valued.

Tell participants to share their thinking process with the customer. Often a salesperson talks about why a customer should buy—but that's only the *product* of the salesperson's thinking. Sharing her or his thinking process with the customer helps gain understanding and alignment on next steps. Talk about how the information the customer provided was used in creating the offer. Sharing the thought process also can reduce the questions a customer might have about the offer.

Encourage the customer to explore the offer. The more a customer explores an offer, the more important information he can obtain. Also, the customer is likely to feel he has more of an investment in the salesperson and the product or service.

9:50   Show slide 12–11. Ask this question: "When would you use the advocacy model?" (**Note to facilitator:** Either have the entire class answer the question, or put the class into pairs to think together on this.) Possible answers include

- when you want to test if the salesperson has enough information to make an offer

- when you want to find out if the customer is ready to make an agreement

- when you want to move into the final negotiation stage

- when you're in a group or formal presentation

- when you want to get the business.

9:55 Show slide 12–12, which outlines the following structured exercise.

Structured Exercise 12–1

Step 1: Split the group into pairs.

Step 2: Have each participant select two or three customers to whom they will present offers in the
next week.

Step 3: Have participants write out their offers using the
advocacy model (put the PowerPoint slide with
the model on the screen or have the model written on a flipchart).

Step 4: Instruct partners to take turns delivering and listening to an offer. Each partner should practice
each offer at least once. The partner listening to
the offer should check for productive advocacy
and provide feedback. Allow 10 minutes.

Step 5: After 10 minutes, have the members of each pair
share what they learned during the exercise.

10:20 Show slide 12–13. The following exercise will help the
participants capture their learning and prepare to use
their new knowledge on the job.

Structured Exercise 12–2

Step 1: Split the class into pairs.

Step 2: Ask each pair to answer the questions on the
slide. Allow 5–10 minutes.

Step 3: Conduct a discussion on topics and challenges.

Option: Ask the participants to write out their answers so
you can give them to their managers for follow-up after
the training.

10:30 Show slide 12–14. Thank the participants for their work
in this module. If you wish, go back to the opening quote
and say that you look forward to the creation of such
compelling offers that the customers simply can't refuse.

What to Do Next

- Review Table 1–1: Sales Training Modules Matrix for help in determining how best to use the module in this chapter and the type of sales personnel who would benefit. Also review the matrix and the sales gap analyses completed by the sales personnel to determine which other modules you might want to use. Finally, review the information in chapter 1 on how best to use this book to fit your situation.

- For the first few modules you facilitate, plan on one hour of preparation for every hour of facilitation. As you gain experience with the modules, plan on 20 minutes of preparation for every hour of facilitation.

- Determine how much time is available for the training session. Schedule the session and arrange for the facility and audiovisual equipment (projector, screen, sound system, computer). Gather any other materials you need

- Determine food and beverage requirements and make necessary arrangements.

- Invite participants and then send confirmation with an agenda or a list of the modules to be covered.

- Practice. Be prepared to respond to questions that the materials and activities are likely to generate. Review the PowerPoint presentation and practice in front of a friend or colleague so that you're comfortable with the key points and slide transitions and have a solid understanding of the topic.

- Decide on the method you will use for splitting the class into working groups (for example, counting off, asking participants to select a partner, and so forth).

- For discussion questions, prepare answers to help participants share their answers (to prime the pump) and use real-life scenarios from your organization.

- As much as possible, check all arrangements in the training room the night before (when training starts in the morning) or two to three hours prior to the start of the session.

- Prepare the evaluation form (see Appendix B) for the attendees so that you can receive feedback and have information for improving the module for future training sessions.

◆ After the session, provide the evaluation results and any post-training assignments to the participants' managers. You also may wish to provide a summary report of any insights you obtained during the training.

◆ ◆ ◆

You've helped your salespeople hone all the skills they need to impress potential clients. All they need now are clients to impress. Chapter 13 presents the tips and techniques they'll use to master the art of effective networking.

Slide 12–1

Compelling Offers

"I made him an offer he couldn't refuse."
- Don Corleone, *Godfather I*

Slide 12–2

Compelling Offers

- **Components of Compelling Offers:**
  - **Conditions of satisfaction**
  - **Customer's language/style**
  - **Alignment and timing**
  - **Collaborative approach**

Slide 12–3

Compelling Offers

A Collaborative Approach through Advocacy

Create a shared understanding and turn words/ideas into coordinated action.

Slide 12–4

Compelling Offers

- **Advocacy Model:**
  - **Own the offer**
  - **Present reasons**
  - **Check for understanding/alignment**
  - **Derive deductions**
  - **Invite responses**

Slide 12–5

Compelling Offers

Examples of Advocacy

- **I think that our upgrade service will provide increased productivity in your call center.**
- **Here are my reasons for stating this:**
  - You have said that the call-center agents find the current software difficult to navigate and that our software is easier to use.
  - Based on the information you kindly shared with me, the wasted productivity of your agents is approximately 30 minutes per agent per day.

Slide 12–6

Compelling Offers

Examples of Advocacy, continued

- **Does my thinking make sense to you?**
- **The implication I see is that you will have a three-month payback period in using our software, based on each agent gaining 20 extra minutes of phone time per day.**
- **I would like to hear your thinking about our offer.**

Slide 12–7

Compelling Offers

Examples of Advocacy

- **The price for the model 1010 is $350.**
- **I am offering this model and the price based on the following reasons:**
  - You requested that the two-year warranty be included in the price and you wished to stay within your budget.
  - The model 1010 provides you with 100% of the features and 20% of the options you have specified.
  - The model 1010 was upgraded this year and has the most current circuitry.

Slide 12–8

Compelling Offers

Example of Advocacy, continued

- **Does my thinking make sense to you?**
- **The benefits of this offer for you are that you stay within budget, you get a machine to handle your needs for at least two years, and the two-year warranty guarantees you no more than 4 hours of downtime.**
- **I think that this is a fair offer and it is important for me to know your thoughts about it.**

Slide 12–9

Compelling Offers

Unproductive Advocacy

- **Don't you agree that...**
- **Don't you think...**
- **Why don't you just try it?**
- **Did you buy that because of X or Y?**

Unproductive advocacy prevents understanding of the customer's position/opinions or, worse, the customer thinks he or she is being manipulated.

Slide 12–10

Compelling Offers

Productive Advocacy

- **Expose your reasoning, data, and concerns.**
- **Use facts as much as possible —***announce any assumptions or opinions.*
- **Share your thinking process—***let the customer participate in your thought process rather than your thought product.*
- **Encourage your customer to inquire about and explore your offer.**

Slide 12–11

Compelling Offers

When would you use
the advocacy model?

Slide 12–12

Practice

- **Select 2–3 customers to whom you will present offers in the next week.**
- **Write out your offer using the advocacy model.**
- **With a partner, practice your offer orally.**
- **Each partner is to practice each offer at least once.**
- **The partner listening to the offer listens for productive advocacy and provides feedback.**

Slide 12–13

Recap

- What have you learned from this module?
- What will you use right away in your work? Why?
- How will you use what you have learned?
- What is an effective way for you to actively improve your offers? Why?
- How will you know your actions are producing results?

Slide 12–14

Compelling Offers

End of the Module

Networking Module

What's in This Chapter?

- A sales module that improves networking skills

- Techniques that aid word-of-mouth advertising

- A description of the six key principles to developing and maintaining an effective network

- An explanation of the theory of six degrees of separation and how it can boost networking efforts

The growth strategy for many organizations is to develop business in new and creative ways. Marketing will continue to drive calls and inquiries through its traditional media efforts and through the Internet. But the number of leads generated in these ways may not achieve the organization's goals. This places pressure on sales personnel to develop their own leads, thus creating a dilemma for a salesforce that already is pressed for time. This is where networking plays an important role. Networks can drive business to the salesperson rather than the salesperson having to search out leads.

Many techniques can help a salesperson generate leads, including leveraging an existing customer base. But the best way, one that ensures the ability to generate leads in the future, is to build an ever-growing network. Many of us think of networking as an art—and it may be. But it's also a science, meaning that a prescribed process can yield a desired result. The deliberate process of networking takes advantage of two major and integrated marketing concepts—word-of-mouth advertising and testimonials.

Word-of-mouth advertising has long been acknowledged as one of the most effective strategies for generating more sales. Think how many times you have purchased in this way and why it works so well.

In word-of-mouth advertising, one person recommends a product or service to a friend or associate. The advocate, who is trusted by the listener, speaks from the perspective of a positive personal experience—whether because of purchase or through a positive relationship—and it becomes a testimonial.

This is a networked world. Professional and personal networks are one way people learn about new things, including products or services they should try. The practice of developing organized networks is growing, particularly because of our ability to maintain communication with hundreds or even thousands of individuals using tools such as databases and the Internet. People still find personal connection in groups, including networking organizations and professional associations. But expanding opportunities, such as knowledge networks, communities of practice, and even eBay hobby communities, all have grown quickly.

Training Objective

The purpose of this module is to provide skills for finding business in today's connected world.

Key Points in This Module

- ◆ Word-of-mouth advertising is the most effective strategy for getting new business.

- ◆ We live in a networked world and there are more opportunities than ever to create connections that drive business leads through referrals and word-of-mouth advertising.

- ◆ There are six key principles to developing and maintaining an effective network.

- ◆ In *Six Degrees of Separation* Stanley Milgram (1967) illustrated how today's communication technologies are shrinking our world.

Materials

- ◆ Two flipchart easels with paper and colored markers

- ◆ LCD projector, screen, and computer for running the PowerPoint presentation

- ◆ A pad of 3 x 5-inch sticky notes for each participant

◆ One marking pen for each participant

◆ Training Instrument 13–1: Networking Worksheet

◆ Tool 13–1: Worksheet Example: Networking

◆ PowerPoint slides 13–1 through 13–16. Copies of the slides for this module, *Networking.ppt,* are included at the end of this chapter.

CD Resources

Materials for this module appear both in this workbook and as electronic files on the CD that accompanies the book. To access the files, insert the CD and look at its "PDF Files" directory for the training instruments and tools need-ed. The PowerPoint presentation is also on the CD. You will find more de-tailed instructions and help in locating files on the CD by referring to Appen-dix C, "Using the Compact Disc," at the back of the workbook.

Sample Agenda

9:00 a.m.   Show slide 13–1. Juan Enriquez is the director of the life sciences project at Harvard Business School and the au-thor of *As the Future Catches You* (2001). In his book he writes about the power of networking through the tech-nology of computers and the Internet. He uses various examples to show how that kind of networking has be-come an integral part of business today. Even the local auto repair shop can create a community of users that forms an expanding network. This module explores tech-niques for setting up and expanding a network.

9:05   Show slide 13–2 (*optional slide*). Read the definition of "networking" to the participants to produce a common understanding of the term.

Show slide 13–3. Let the participants know that the the-ory of six degrees of separation illustrates how small our world is with existing communications technology and the power of networks.

If you wonder why networks are so powerful, think of the origin of the term "six degrees of separation." In the 1960s psychologist Stanley Milgram conducted an experiment

Table 13–1

Slide Information for the Networking Module

NUMBER	TITLE	DESCRIPTION	TIME
13–1	Title slide: Networking	Lets the class get settled and lets the facilitator welcome the group as appropriate	2–5 minutes
13–2	Definition	Definition of the term "networking" (optional)	1 minute
13–3	Six degrees of separation	Example of the power of networks	3 minutes
13–4	What networks do we already participate in?	Discussion question	3 minutes
13–5	Key principles	Overview of six principles	1 minute
13–6	Give	Detail of the principle	1 minute
13–7	Trust	Detail of the principle	1 minute
13–8	Invest	Detail of the principle	1 minute
13–9	Embrace	Detail of the principle	1 minute
13–10	Master	Detail of the principle	1 minute
13–11	Energize	Detail of the principle	1 minute
13–12	NetWORK	Networking takes work and discipline	1 minute
13–13	Practice	Structured exercise	5–10 minutes
13–14	Practice	Structured exercise, continued	10–15 minutes
13–15	Recap	Structured exercise	10–15 minutes
13–16	End of the module		

to discover how people are connected. He started a chain letter by mailing packets to 160 people in Omaha, Nebraska. The packet contained the instructions for creating the chain, including the name and address of the intended end recipient, a stockbroker who lived in Sharon, Massachusetts, and worked in Boston. These were the instructions: "Simply write your name on the packet (as a tracking device). Mail the packet to a friend or acquaintance who is likely to get it closer to the intended final recipient." In other words, each handler could only mail it to someone in his or her own existing network.

In the 1960s, written correspondence was the primary means of communication outside our respective local calling areas. Long-distance telephone was used sparingly because of expense and convention. Obviously, electronic media did not exist for the everyday user. Most people didn't have a network that was spread broadly across the globe as is possible today. Most of those 160 people probably knew relatively few people—by today's standards—outside their local communities, much less specifically closer to Massachusetts.

Amazingly, Milgram found that most of the packets reached their destination in five or six steps. Hence the term "six degrees of separation." Milgram demonstrated that this is, indeed, a small world.

Fast-forward to the present: With the kind of connectivity we have today, salespeople are only a degree or two away from a vast network of customers. The only question is how to tap that network effectively and make it produce business. The challenge is not only in the ways to make connections with the right people. The difficulty of networking is in the time and discipline it requires to cultivate and nurture our networks so they produce the fruit we need.

9:10 Show slide 13–4. Ask the group the following discussion question: "What are the different networks you already have?" Write their answers on a flipchart.

9:15 Show slide 13–5. Introduce the following key principles of networking:

- ◆ give

- ◆ trust

- ◆ invest

- ◆ embrace
- ◆ master
- ◆ energize.

Show slide 13–6. Tell the class that the main networking activity should be to *give* something of value to individuals and to one's networks. Some examples of adding value are

- ◆ helping people in the network make timely and beneficial connections
- ◆ offering qualified advice or ideas
- ◆ sharing knowledge by emailing news or articles of interest
- ◆ supporting people in times of need.

Key actions include

- ◆ focusing on giving more than you ever hope to receive
- ◆ separating giving from receiving; don't ask for anything in the same interaction in which you are giving.

9:20   Show slide 13–7. Say that *trust* works here in two ways:

1.   You must trust the process of building your network.

2.   You must realize that it takes time to build trust in the relationships you cultivate in your network.

9:25   Show slide 13–8. Tell the participants that *investing* time to truly connect, to get to know people, and to create real relationships is key. People sense when others are being authentic, and networks don't grow out of superficial relationships.

9:30   Show slide 13–9. Say that it is important to be inclusive and gracious—*embracing*—in every interaction you have. You never know when or with whom opportunity will knock!

Be open to and ready for opportunities when they present themselves. Every time you go to a public place or answer the phone, be mentally prepared to interact graciously and generously.

9:35   Show slide 13–10. Tell the group it is important to become known for something and become the sparkling center of your networks. In his book *The Tipping Point*, Malcolm Gladwell identifies those he calls "mavens"—people who have reliable information on one or more topics. Even without being an expert on any particular subject, you can become a hub by expertly connecting people who seek information with those who have it. Be a connector! Gladwell defines connectors as people who have a "special gift for bringing the world together." Although it seems that some people come by this talent naturally, connecting also can be a skill that you can master.

9:40   Show slide 13–11. Ask the group this question: "Have you ever noticed how a compliment or your positive attitude caused someone to brighten up?" People naturally are attracted to those who are positive and optimistic and who exude energy. The more energy you produce, the more people will seek you out—even strangers who could lead you to windfalls.

9:45   Show slide 13–12. Make the key point that the value of effective networking is not necessarily apparent until a salesperson starts to reap the rewards. In the meantime, networking is hard work and requires discipline to maintain daily and weekly activities while waiting for results. There are routines that will help salespeople network more consistently and effectively. Here are some points to stress with your participants:

◆ Networking is hard but fulfilling work.

◆ It takes enthusiasm and discipline.

◆ It is critical that salespeople plan for the activities and tasks that build networks.

◆ They should continue to explore ways to integrate networking activities into the routines that are driven by a schedule or by their task list.

9:50   Show slides 13–13 and 13–14, which outline the following structured exercise.

Structured Exercise 13–1

Step 1: Using 3 x 5-inch sticky notes, each participant should write one idea per page about the different networks that are available to him or her.

Step 2: Collect the notes and post them on a wall or flipchart. Some of the ideas that people will come up with include chambers of commerce, trade associations, and clubs. Let them be creative with ideas.

Step 3: After about five minutes, when all ideas are posted, ask the class to review the ideas and sort them by priority.

Step 4: Identify the top 10 ideas for the next part of the exercise.

Step 5: Each participant selects the network he or she want to join. It's fine for a salesperson to choose a network to which she or he already belongs.

Step 6: Split the class into pairs.

Step 7: Pass out copies of Training Instrument 13–1 and Tool 13–1. Ask everyone to complete the worksheet for the network they selected. (**Note to facilitator:** Display slide 13–5 as a reminder about key principles for networking that should be built into participants' plans.)

Step 8: After 10–15 minutes have the pairs orally share their worksheets with the class.

10:05   Show slide 13–15, which outlines the following structured exercise.

Structured Exercise 13–2

Note to facilitator: In the following exercise you will help the participants capture learning and prepare to use their new knowledge on the job.

Step 1: Ask each pair to work together to answer the questions on the slide.

Step 2: After 10–15 minutes have each pair share its answers.

Option: Ask the participants to write out their answers so you can give them to their managers for follow-up after the training.

10:30   Show slide 13–16. Thank the participants for attending this module and let them know that you look forward to hearing how they have grown their networks.

What to Do Next

- Review Table 1–1: Sales Training Modules Matrix for help in determining how best to use the module in this chapter and the type of sales personnel who would benefit. Also review the matrix and the sales gap analyses completed by the sales personnel to determine which other modules you might want to use. Finally, review the information in chapter 1 on how best to use this book to fit your situation.

- For the first few modules you facilitate, plan on one hour of preparation for every hour of facilitation. As you gain experience with the modules, plan on 20 minutes of preparation for every hour of facilitation.

- Determine how much time is available for the training session. Schedule the session and arrange for the facility and audiovisual equipment (projector, screen, sound system, computer). Gather whatever other materials you will need.

- Determine food and beverage requirements and make necessary arrangements.

- Invite participants. Send confirmation with an agenda or a list of the modules to be covered.

- Prepare copies of training materials to match your enrollment.

- Practice. Carefully review the training materials. Be prepared to respond to questions that the materials and activities are likely to generate. Review the PowerPoint presentation and practice in front of a friend or colleague so you are comfortable with the key points and slide transitions and have a solid understanding of the topic.

◆ Choose the method you will use for splitting the class into working groups (for example, counting off, asking everyone to select a partner, and so forth).

◆ For discussion questions, prepare answers to help participants share their answers (to prime the pump) and use real-life scenarios from your organization.

◆ As much as possible, check all arrangements in the training room the night before (when training starts in the morning) or two to three hours prior to the start of the session.

◆ Prepare the evaluation form (see Appendix B) for the attendees so that you can receive feedback and have information for improving the module for future training sessions.

◆ After the session, provide the evaluation results and any post-training assignments to the participants' managers. You also may wish to provide a summary report of any insights you obtained during the training.

Training Instrument 13–1
Networking Worksheet

Networking strategies

1. _____

2. _____

3. _____

Tactics . . . first steps

1. _____

2. _____

3. _____

4. _____

5. _____

The ways I will measure success

1. _____

2. _____

3. _____

4. _____

5. _____

Tool 13–1

Worksheet Example: Networking

Networking strategies

1. Get more business from current customers

2. Join XYZ club

Tactics . . . first steps

1. *Segment current customers into three groups (used us in past three months; used us in past six months; and more than nine months since they used us); send a customized email to each and set up a trace system to send articles or other value-added communications.*

2. *Find out the cost of joining XYZ club and get budget approval. After joining, select a committee to join, such as membership, and become active in the club.*

The ways I will measure success

1. *Keep track of the responses I get from customers to my communications and keep track of how many customers increase their number of purchases.*

2. *I get accepted to a committee within three months of joining. After six months I have five strong relationships going. Before nine months I have at least three referrals for business and one purchase.*

Slide 13–1

Networking

*"Now you do not need a business...or fortune
to set up a very large network....
Just word of mouth."*

– Juan Enriquez

Slide 13–2

Networking

Definition:

The exchange of information or
services among individuals, groups,
or institutions; *specifically*, the
cultivation of productive
relationships for... business.

Slide 13–3

Networking

Six Degrees of Separation

- 1960s psychologist Stanley Milgram conducted an experiment.
- 160 packets were sent by people in Omaha, Nebraska.
- Recipients were instructed to mail the packet to a friend or acquaintance who is likely to get it closer to the intended recipient in Boston.
- Most of the packets reached the final destination in five or six steps.
- All of this occurred before there were faxes or email!

Slide 13–4

Networking

What networks
do you already participate in?

Slide 13–5

Networking

Key Principles for Networking:
- Give
- Trust
- Invest
- Embrace
- Master
- Energize

Slide 13–6

Networking

Give

- Outflow value to individuals and the network.
- Focus on giving more than you ever hope to receive.
- Separate giving from receiving.

Slide 13–7

Networking

Trust

- Trust that the process works.
- Realize that it takes time to build trust.

Slide 13–8

Networking

Invest
- Take time to truly connect.
- Get to know people.
- Create real relationships.

Slide 13–9

Networking

Embrace
- Be inclusive.
- Be gracious.
- Be open and ready when opportunity knocks.

Slide 13–10

Networking

Master
- Become known for something.
- Be the sparkling center of your networks.

Slide 13–11

Networking

Energize
- The more energy you flow out, the more people will be attracted to you.

Slide 13–12

Networking

NetWORK

- Hard and fulfilling work
- Enthusiasm and discipline
- Plan
- Explore

Slide 13–13

Practice

- On the notepad you have, write one idea on one note about the different networks that are available.
- Your facilitator will place the notes on the wall.
- As a class, review all the ideas and select the top 10 ideas.

Slide 13–14

Practice

- From the top 10 ideas, select which networks you would like to join.
- With a partner and using the Networking Worksheet, develop
  - networking strategies
  - tactics... first steps
  - measurements of success.
- Share your worksheets with the class.

Slide 13–15

Recap

- What have you learned from this module?
- What will you use right away in your work? Why?
- How will you use what you have learned?
- What is an effective way for you to actively improve your networking skills? Why?
- How will you know your actions are producing results?

Slide 13–16

Networking

End of the Module

Training Program Examples

These are example programs for one or more days and they follow a logical order to support successive modules.

For multiple-day programs the following combinations can be made:

* Programs A and B can be combined into a two-day program for new salespeople.

* Programs A, B, and C can be combined into a three-day program for new salespeople.

* Programs D and E can be combined into a two-day program for experienced salespeople or for a mixed group.

* Programs D, E, and C can be combined into a three-day program for experienced salespeople or for a mixed group.

Table A–1

One-Day Program A—Novice Salespeople

TIME	MODULE/ACTIVITY	DURATION	WHERE TO FIND IN THE WORKBOOK
9:00 a.m.	Welcome and Check-in (introductions and expectations for the training)	15 minutes	Chapter 1, page 6
9:15 a.m.	Selling Today	30 minutes	Chapter 3, page 34
9:45 a.m.	Effective Selling	30 minutes	Chapter 3, page 38
10:15 a.m.	Break	15 minutes	
10:30 a.m.	Sales Cycles	1 hour	Chapter 3, page 42
11:30 a.m.	Basic Knowledge	1 hour	Chapter 3, page 49
12:30 p.m.	Lunch	1.5 hours	
2:00 p.m.	Sales Mind Focus	1.25 hours	Chapter 4, page 77
3:15 p.m.	Break	15 minutes	
3:30 p.m.	Managing Tasks and Relationships	45 minutes	Chapter 5, page 91
4:15 p.m.	Conditions of Satisfaction	45 minutes	Chapter 6, page 109
5:00 p.m.	Check-out	15 minutes	Chapter 1, page 6

Table A–2

One-Day Program B—Novice Salespeople

TIME	MODULE/ACTIVITY	DURATION	WHERE TO FIND IN THE WORKBOOK
9:00 a.m.	Welcome and Check-in (introductions and expectations for the training)	15 minutes	Chapter 1, page 6
9:15 a.m.	Artful Listening	45 minutes	Chapter 8, page 132
10:00 a.m.	Break	15 minutes	
10:15 a.m.	Inquiry	1 hour	Chapter 8, page 137
11:15 a.m.	Break	15 minutes	
11:30 a.m.	Inquiry, continued	30 minutes	Chapter 8, page 137
Noon	Lunch	1.5 hours	
1:30 p.m.	Communicating—A Basic Formula	1 hour	Chapter 9, page 159
2:30 p.m.	Break	15 minutes	
2:45 p.m.	Communicating—A Basic Formula, continued	30 minutes	Chapter 9, page 159
3:45 p.m.	Networking	1 hour	Chapter 13, page 229
4:45 p.m.	Check-out	15 minutes	Chapter 1, page 6

Table A–3

One-Day Program C—Experienced Salespeople or Mixed Group

TIME	MODULE/ACTIVITY	DURATION	WHERE TO FIND IN THE WORKBOOK
9:00 a.m.	Welcome and Check-in (introductions and expectations for the training)	15 minutes	Chapter 1, page 6
9:15 a.m.	Features, Benefits, Proof	1 hour	Chapter 11, page 203
10:15 a.m.	Break	15 minutes	
10:30 a.m.	Compelling Offers	1 hour	Chapter 12, page 215
11:30 a.m.	Break	15 minutes	
11:45 a.m.	Presentations	45 minutes	Chapter 10, page 189
12:30 p.m.	Lunch	1.5 hours	
2:00 p.m.	Presentations, continued	1 hour	Chapter 10, page 189
3:00 p.m.	Break	15 minutes	
3:15 p.m.	Review of all modules trained to date	1 hour	
4:15 p.m.	Check-out	15 minutes	Chapter 1, page 6

Table A–4

One-Day Program D—Experienced Salespeople or Mixed Group

TIME	MODULE/ACTIVITY	DURATION	WHERE TO FIND IN THE WORKBOOK
9:00 a.m.	Welcome and Check-in (introductions and expectations for the training)	15 minutes	Chapter 1, page 6
9:15 a.m.	Sales Mind Focus	1.25 hours	Chapter 4, page 77
10:30 a.m.	Break	15 minutes	
10:45 a.m.	Managing Tasks and Relationships	45 minutes	Chapter 5, page 91
11:30 a.m.	Break	15 minutes	
11:45 a.m.	Conditions of Satisfaction	45 minutes	Chapter 6, page 109
12:30 p.m.	Lunch	1.5 hours	
2:00 p.m.	Planning and Organizing	1 hour	Chapter 7, page 119
3:00 p.m.	Break	15 minutes	
3:15 p.m.	Networking	1 hour	Chapter 13, page 229
4:15 p.m.	Check-out	15 minute	Chapter 1, page 6

Table A–5

One-Day Program E—Experienced Salespeople or Mixed Group

TIME	MODULE/ACTIVITY	DURATION	WHERE TO FIND IN THE WORKBOOK
9:00 a.m.	Welcome and Check-in (introductions and expectations for the training)	15 minutes	Chapter 1, page 6
9:15 a.m.	Artful Listening	45 minutes	Chapter 8, page 132
10:00 a.m.	Break	15 minutes	
10:15 a.m.	Inquiry	1 hour	Chapter 8, page 137
11:15 a.m.	Break	15 minutes	
11:30 a.m.	Inquiry, continued	30 minutes	Chapter 8, page 137
Noon	Lunch	1.5 hours	
1:30 p.m.	Communicating—A Basic Formula	1 hour	Chapter 9, page 159
2:30 p.m.	Break	15 minutes	
2:45 p.m.	Communicating—A Basic Formula, continued	1 hour	Chapter 9, page 159
3:45 p.m.	Check-out	15 minutes	Chapter 1, page 6

Program Evaluation Form

	UNACCEPTABLE	NOT VERY GOOD	GOOD	VERY GOOD	EXCELLENT
PROGRAM OBJECTIVE					
Program objective was achieved	☐	☐	☐	☐	☐
Program objective met my expectations	☐	☐	☐	☐	☐

Comments:

	UNACCEPTABLE	NOT VERY GOOD	GOOD	VERY GOOD	EXCELLENT
PROGRAM CONTENT					
Subject(s) were adequately covered	☐	☐	☐	☐	☐
I learned new things	☐	☐	☐	☐	☐
Applicable on-the-job	☐	☐	☐	☐	☐

Comments:

	UNACCEPTABLE	NOT VERY GOOD	GOOD	VERY GOOD	EXCELLENT
PROGRAM LEADER'S PERFORMANCE					
Had sufficient knowledge of the subject	☐	☐	☐	☐	☐
Created a positive environment	☐	☐	☐	☐	☐
Clearly communicated concepts	☐	☐	☐	☐	☐
Presented program in an interesting manner	☐	☐	☐	☐	☐
Provided guidance during the program	☐	☐	☐	☐	☐
Engaged my participation	☐	☐	☐	☐	☐

Comments:

Continued on next page

Ideas and suggestions to improve the program in the future:

_____

_____

_____

_____

_____

_____

_____

_____

_____

Additional comments:

_____

_____

_____

_____

_____

_____

_____

_____

_____

◆

Using the Compact Disc

Insert the CD and locate the file *How to Use This CD.txt.*

Contents of the CD

The compact disc that accompanies this workbook on sales training contains three types of files. All of the files can be used on a variety of computer platforms.

- ◆ **Adobe .pdf documents.** These include assessments, figures, tables, tools, and training instruments.

- ◆ **Microsoft PowerPoint presentations.** These presentations add interest and depth to many of the training activities included in the workbook.

- ◆ **Microsoft PowerPoint files of overhead transparency masters.** These files makes it easy to print viewgraphs and handouts in black-and-white rather than using an office copier. They contain only text and line drawings; there are no images to print in grayscale.

Computer Requirements

To read or print the .pdf files on the CD, you must have Adobe Acrobat Reader software installed on your system. The program can be downloaded free of cost from the Adobe Website, *www.adobe.com.*

To use or adapt the contents of the PowerPoint presentation files on the CD, you must have Microsoft PowerPoint software installed on your system. If you simply want to view the PowerPoint documents, you must have an appropriate viewer installed on your system. Microsoft provides various viewers free for downloading from its Website, *www.microsoft.com*.

Printing From the CD

TEXT FILES

You can print the training materials using Adobe Acrobat Reader. Simply open the .pdf file and print as many copies as you need. The following .pdf documents can be directly printed from the CD:

- Assessment 2–1: Sales Gap Analysis—Knowledge

- Assessment 2–2: Sales Gap Analysis—Sales Mind Focus

- Assessment 2–3: Sales Gap Analysis—Managing Tasks and Relationships

- Assessment 2–4: Sales Gap Analysis—Conditions of Satisfaction

- Assessment 2–5: Sales Gap Analysis—Listening, Inquiry, and Advocacy

- Assessment 2–6: Sales Gap Analysis—Communicating

- Assessment 2–7: Sales Gap Analysis—Benefits

- Assessment 2–8: Sales Gap Analysis—Networking

- Figure 2–1: Willing and Able Matrix

- Table 1–1: Sales Training Modules Matrix

- Table 1–2: Half-Day Training Session for Novice Salespeople

- Table 1–3: Half-Day Training Session for Experienced Salespeople

- Table 1–4: Full-Day Training Program A

- Table 1–5: Full-Day Training Program B

- Table 3–1: Slide Information for the Selling Today Module

- Table 3–2: Slide Information for the Effective Selling Module

- Table 3–3: Slide Information for the Sales Cycle Module

- Table 4–1: Slide Information for the Sales Mind Focus Module

- Table 5–1: Slide Information for the Managing Tasks and Relationships Module
- Table 6–1: Slide Information for the Conditions of Satisfaction Module
- Table 7–1: Slide Information for the Planning and Organizing Module
- Table 8–1: Slide Information for the Artful Listening Module
- Table 8–2: Slide Information for the Inquiry Module
- Table 9–1: Slide Information for the Communicating: A Basic Formula Module
- Table 10–1: Slide Information for the Presentations Module
- Table 11–1: Slide Information for the Features, Benefits, and Proof Module
- Table 12–1: Slide Information for the Compelling Offers Module
- Table 13–1: Slide Information for the Networking Module
- Table A–1: One-Day Program A—Novice Salespeople
- Table A–2: One-Day Program B—Novice Salespeople
- Table A–3: One-Day Program C—Experienced Salespeople
- Table A–4: One-Day Program D—Experienced Salespeople
- Table A–5: One-Day Program E—Experienced Salespeople
- Tool 2–1: Knowledge Gap Analysis
- Tool 3–1: Worksheet Example A: Product Knowledge
- Tool 3–2: Worksheet Example B: Product Knowledge
- Tool 3–3: Worksheet Example: Competitor Knowledge
- Tool 3–4: Worksheet Example: Top Competitors Summary
- Tool 3–5: Worksheet Example: Individual and Corporate Customer Knowledge
- Tool 7–1: Worksheet Example: Where Does My Time Go?
- Tool 8–1: Qualification Questions
- Tool 8–2: Understanding the Customer Questions

- Tool 8–3: Conditions of Satisfaction Questions

- Tool 8–4: Asking for the Business Questions

- Tool 9–1: Worksheet Example: Communicating in Person

- Tool 9–2: Worksheet Example: Communicating by Telephone

- Tool 9–3: Worksheet Example: Communicating in Writing by Email

- Tool 10–1: Worksheet Example: Presentation

- Tool 11–1: Worksheet Example: Features, Benefits, and Proof

- Tool 13–1: Worksheet Example: Networking

- Training Instrument 3–1: Product Knowledge Worksheet

- Training Instrument 3–2: Competitor Knowledge Worksheet

- Training Instrument 3–3: Top Competitors Summary Worksheet

- Training Instrument 3–4: Individual and Corporate Customer Knowledge Worksheet

- Training Instrument 7–1: Where Does My Time Go? Worksheet

- Training Instrument 9–1: Worksheet: Communicating in Person

- Training Instrument 9–2: Worksheet: Communicating by Telephone

- Training Instrument 9–3: Worksheet: Communicating in Writing by Letter, Email, or Fax

- Training Instrument 10–1: Presentation Worksheet

- Training Instrument 11–1: Features, Benefits, and Proof Worksheet

- Training Instrument 13–1: Networking Worksheet

- Program Evaluation Form

POWERPOINT SLIDES

You can print the presentation slides directly from this CD using Microsoft PowerPoint. Simply open the .ppt files and print as many copies as you need. You can also make handouts of the presentations by printing 2, 4, or 6 "slides" per page. These slides will be in color, with design elements embedded. PowerPoint also permits you to print these in grayscale or black-and-white, although printing from the overhead masters file will yield better black-and-white representations. Many trainers who use personal computers to project their presentations bring along viewgraphs just in case there are glitches in the system. The overhead masters can be printed from the PowerPoint .pps files.

Adapting the PowerPoint Slides

You can modify or otherwise customize the slides by opening and editing them in the appropriate application. However, you must retain the denotation of the original source of the material—it is illegal to pass it off as your own work. You may indicate that a document was adapted from this workbook, written by Jim Mikula and copyrighted by ASTD and Customer Contact Corporation. The files will open as "Read Only," so before you adapt them you will need to save them onto your hard drive under a different file name.

Showing the PowerPoint Presentations

On the CD, the following PowerPoint presentations are included:

- ◆ Selling Today.ppt
- ◆ Effective Selling.ppt
- ◆ Sales Cycles.ppt
- ◆ Sales Mind Focus.ppt
- ◆ Managing Tasks and Relationships.ppt
- ◆ Conditions of Satisfaction.ppt
- ◆ Planning and Organizing.ppt
- ◆ Artful Listening.ppt
- ◆ Inquiry.ppt
- ◆ Basic Formula.ppt
- ◆ Presentations.ppt
- ◆ Features and Benefits.ppt
- ◆ Compelling Offers.ppt
- ◆ Networking.

Having the presentations in .ppt format means that they automatically show full-screen when you double-click on a file name. You also can open Microsoft PowerPoint and launch the presentations from there.

Table C–1

Navigating Through a PowerPoint Presentation

KEY	POWERPOINT "SHOW" ACTION
Space bar *or* Enter *or* Mouse click	Advance through custom animations embedded in the presentation
Backspace	Back up to the last projected element of the presentation
Escape	Abort the presentation
B *or* b	Blank the screen to black
B *or* b *(repeat)*	Resume the presentation
W *or* w	Blank the screen to white
W *or* w *(repeat)*	Resume the presentation

Use the space bar, the enter key, or mouse clicks to advance through a show. Press the backspace key to back up. Use the escape key to abort a presentation. If you want to blank the screen to black while the group discusses a point, press the B key. Pressing it again restores the show. If you want to blank the screen to a white background, do the same with the W key. Table C–1 summarizes these instructions.

We strongly recommend that trainers practice making presentations before using them in training situations. You should be confident that you can cogently expand on the points featured in the presentations and discuss the methods for working through them. If you want to engage your training participants fully (rather than worrying about how to show the next slide), become familiar with this simple technology *before* you need to use it. A good practice is to insert notes into the *Speaker's Notes* feature of the PowerPoint program, print them out, and have them in front of you when you present the slides.

For Further Reading

Enriquez, Juan. 2001. *As the Future Catches You: How Genomics & Other Forces Are Changing Your Life, Work, Health, and Wealth*. New York: Crown Business.

Farber, Barry J., and Joyce Wycoff. 1992. *Break-Through Selling: Customer-Building Strategies from the Best in the Business*. Englewood Cliffs, NJ: Prentice Hall.

Gladwell, Malcolm. *The Tipping Point*. New York: Little, Brown, 2000.

Mackay, Harvey. *Dig Your Well Before You're Thirsty: The Only Networking Book You'll Ever Need*. New York: Doubleday Books, 1997.

Milgram, Stanley. The Small World Problem. 1967. *Psychology Today* I: 60–67.

Rackham, Neil, and John R. Devincentis. *Rethinking the Sales Force: Redefining Selling to Create and Capture Customer Value*. New York: McGraw-Hill, 1999.

Willingham, Ron. *Integrity Selling for the 21st Century: How to Sell the Way People Want to Buy*. New York: Currency/Doubleday, 2003.

Jim Mikula's varied professional background began with 10 years in sales and marketing at the Hyatt and Sheraton hotel chains. With a move to Asia in 1988, Mikula headed up sales and marketing for the Regent and Four Seasons hotels. After investing extraordinary efforts serving as director of marketing in those venues, by 1996 Mikula became the regional director of field marketing and then area director of marketing in India. He set up regional sales offices and reservations systems in all areas, and designed and developed an overall sales and marketing strategy for India, including worldwide public relations and advertising.

Throughout his career, Mikula has been recognized for his affable way with people and his excellent leadership skills. His success is traceable to his natural adaptability and creativity in new situations. He has a personal commitment to lifelong learning that expresses itself through curiosity and an instinct to challenge assumptions, explore innovation, and search for possibilities. With Customer Contact Corporation (C^3) since 1999, he brings solid corporate experience and cutting edge knowledge to C^3's clients.

Community service is also important to Mikula, and his efforts have included managing the protocols for Pope John Paul II's 1987 visit to Miami, chairing four major cancer-research fundraising runs, and lecturing at colleges and universities worldwide.

The ASTD Trainer's WorkShop Series is designed to be a practical, hands-on road map to help you quickly develop training in key business areas. Each book in the series offers all the exercises, handouts, assessments, structured experiences, and ready-to-use presentations needed to develop effective training sessions. In addition to easy-to-use icons, each book in the series includes a companion CD-ROM with PowerPoint presentations and electronic copies of all supporting material featured in the book.

Other books in the Trainer's WorkShop Series:

- ◆ *New Supervisor Training*
  John E. Jones and Chris W. Chen

- ◆ *Customer Service Training*
  Maxine Kamin

- ◆ *New Employee Orientation Training*
  Karen Lawson

- ◆ *Leading Change Training*
  Jeffrey Russell and Linda Russell

- ◆ *Leadership Training*
  Lou Russell

- ◆ *Coaching Training*
  Chris W. Chen

- ◆ *Project Management Training*
  Bill Shackelford

- ◆ *Innovation Training*
  Ruth Ann Hattori and Joyce Wycoff